House, Home and Society

Rowland Atkinson is author of:

Securing an Urban Renaissance (with Gesa Helms, eds.)
Shades of Deviance (ed.)
Gated Communities, International Perspectives (with Sarah Blandy, eds.)
Domestic Fortress (with Sarah Blandy)

Keith Jacobs is author of:

The Dynamics of Local Housing Policy
Social Constructionism in Housing Research (with Jim Kemeny and Tony Manzi, eds.)
Experience and Representation: Contemporary Perspectives on Migration in Australia
Ocean To Outback: Cosmpolitanism in Contemporary Australia (with Jeff Malpas, eds.)

House, Home and Society

Rowland Atkinson
Professor, University of Sheffield, UK

Keith Jacobs
Professor, University of Tasmania, Australia

First published 2016 by
PALGRAVE

Palgrave in the UK is an imprint of Macmillan Publishers Limited, registered in England, company number 785998, of 4 Crinan Street, London, N1 9XW.

Palgrave is a global imprint of the above companies and is represented throughout the world.

Palgrave® and Macmillan® are registered trademarks in the United States, the United Kingdom, Europe and other countries.

ISBN 978–1–137–29403–6 hardback
ISBN 978–1–137–29402–9 paperback

This book is printed on paper suitable for recycling and made from fully managed and sustained forest sources. Logging, pulping, and manufacturing processes are expected to conform to the environmental regulations of the country of origin.

A catalogue record for this book is available from the British Library.

A catalog record for this book is available from the Library of Congress.

Printed and bound by CPI Group (UK) Ltd, Croydon, CR0 4YY

Contents

List of Figures and Tables

Figures

Tables

Acknowledgments

The observations and questions of our students have helped us to shape the form and content of this book, and we would like to acknowledge their contribution here. We would also like to thank Lloyd Langman, Nicola Cattini, and Tuur Driesser at Palgrave for their fabulous editorial support while writing this book, and Peter Somerville, Peter King, and an anonymous reviewer for their very helpful suggestions on a first draft. We are also grateful to the support provided to Keith Jacobs by the Australian Research Council's Future Fellowship Award FT120100471.

1 House, Home and Society

Introduction

In many ways, the private home is a window on the social world around us. It is a private space for personal expression, a place to escape from a sometimes-hostile world, and a place that helps us to maintain our well-being and the economic security of both those in our household and ourselves (Blunt and Dowling, 2006). In a rather primal sense, our home is the means by which we are able to stay safe, sheltered, and well; it plays a central role in binding various aspects of our lives together by offering a place of sanctuary and a primary place to which we can retreat and literally find a home (King, 2004). Life without it is quite simply unthinkable, and to experience life or some part of it without a home is almost unbearable, as those who experience such a situation report (Cloke, May, and Johnsen, 2010). As the sociologist Peter Saunders (1990) once remarked, home is

> where people feel in control of the environment, free from surveillance, free to be themselves and at ease, in the deepest psychological sense, in a world that might at times be experienced as threatening and uncontrollable. (p. 361)

Without a home, the critical building block of family and its diverse forms becomes impossible, and without these distinctive physical structures, societies would neither function nor exist. In this sense, what we call society is co-determined and fundamentally related to the nature, scale, structures, and forms of the built, domestic environment and human construction efforts. Social life passes through, is mediated by, and ultimately structured in subtle ways by the buildings we inhabit as homes and the array of other constructions around us that we may visit on a daily basis. These spaces and the dwellings we inhabit structure us, assist us, and shape the pathways and flow of our daily lives. It is then rather surprising that the study of housing has not been a central focus in the social sciences. Few courses, almost no textbooks, and arguably a specialized preoccupation by researchers form the basis of interest in the home. Yet, like the study of cities, our interest in housing has a long pedigree of theoretical and empirical concerns in society, modernity, political economy, and other primary elements of a sociological perspective. Massive economic transformations and the emergence of mass consumer societies, followed by postmodern and post-industrial social formations that have changed the way we relate to each other and go about our everyday lives, can all be linked to the nature and provision of housing for different social groups, to the growing urban centers of the industrial metropolis, and to later concerns about a range of social problems. These stories of social change, our economic history, and politics can be mapped onto the traditional mainstays of sociological analysis—the relationships between modern society, housing and urban form (Savage and Warde, 1993).

This book is an attempt to make housing a clear area of study for students and to help make sense of empirical and theoretical scholarship in this area. Rarely has the home been identified as a pivotal focus in a subdiscipline of sociology, and it has often been left to researchers from diverse disciplines to develop the field known as housing studies (which we use here as a shorthand to describe the range of theoretical and empirical efforts at profiling and understanding the home) and to take seriously the place of homes within societies, cities, political systems and economies. This book moves toward articulating the scope of the sociology of housing to shed light on contemporary societal values, policy challenges and demographic changes that, in combination, continue to influence the way we live.

The home in context

Many assumptions we make about homes are linked to cultural or national reference points. For example, in much of the Global North, owning a home is commonly perceived to be an important rite of passage through life, offering us feelings of security because of the economic stake in it. In Australia, home ownership is referred to as the Australian dream and is a major aspect of personal and national elements of social identity formation (Kemeny, 1983; Allon, 2008). The very idea that the home is a private, sacrosanct space is often given form in expressions like "an Englishman's home is his castle" (a notion which sees similar expression in other cultures, like that of the United States, where control and defense are central to many laws). These values of privacy and self-determination retain a powerful hold on the collective imagination. In contrast, in countries within the former Soviet bloc and other post-communist societies, the universal provision of homes for rent was nevertheless often seen as a shelter from prying eyes and agents of the state (Heinen, 1997). With the advent of markets in these societies over the past twenty years, society has also changed, with newfound social freedoms set against problems of quality and affordability. These changes reveal how the multiple meanings and roles of the home are shaped by social forces within particular national and regional contexts.

As we will continue to argue in this book, particular historical economic and political conditions shape cultures and social values. Not only do these critical forces influence the production, experience, and meaning of homes, but these same outcomes also feed back to shape the values of entire cultures. For example, in the United States and the United Kingdom, it is possible to talk of a culture of ownership, but what does this really mean—that the British share some core values and aspirations of ownership? What are the social and economic forces that might generate such values? A key element of such apparently shared values has been the role of successive governments that have, in order to become politically popular, sought to help many people become owners. Yet the promotion of what many perceive as a natural tenure has come to mean that many people see ownership as natural and renting as a form of social deviation (Rowlands and Gurney, 2000). In much of mainland Europe (such as The Netherlands), renting one's home from the state and private landlords is not only much more popular but also stems from the better regulation and the historically specific role of governments mandated to provide good-quality homes for citizens. In this sense, buying a home is not natural, inevitable, or always desirable.

Where and how we live are fundamentally influenced by forces that are largely out of our control. These can be highlighted by considering how economic conditions in the past decade or so, under a global recession, have helped to generate increasing levels of economic inequality, job insecurity and the repossession of homes. Following many decades of a steady rise in home ownership in countries like the United States and the United Kingdom, access to ownership has now fallen dramatically, particularly for younger people. These new risks, of repossession, default, and even homelessness, help demonstrate how our home and its relative stability are critical to us; new forms of precariousness in our work lives highlight this. We will return to the realization that our housing tenure, whether we find ourselves owning or renting our home (either from a private or public landlord), is an important influence that deeply shapes us and affects the opportunities and deficits we experience in life (such as the quality of local services and our exposure to risks like crime).

The societies of which we are inseparably a part flow into the spaces of the home (Miller, 1988) through its interior daily social life via the codes of conduct and social norms reproduced by parents among their children (Morgan, 2013) or via the screens and windows that offer perspectives on the world outside (Bignell, 2012). This sense of the home as a fundamental node within spaces and networks of social interaction and communication has major influence on our values and tastes, and also shapes the way we inhabit and decorate the home. Fears and anxieties about global crises, crime, social problems, and the risks associated with going beyond the threshold of the front door have an impact on the patterns and daily flow of our lives and give the notion that it is a territory under threat, both in and outside the home (Atkinson and Blandy, 2007). Perhaps even more importantly, our home is the main space in which social reproduction occurs—the place in which children are reared and which contains the building blocks of social life that shape us as individuals, households, families, couples, and individual occupiers of the home; and thereby wider social institutions, where possibilities are remade and built over time. As we discuss later, these factors are the focus of feelings of personal joy and strong feelings of social escape and self-determination; they also offer theorists great scope to consider how and why individuals are brought into society and made in "its" image, and about the formation of dominant ideas and powerful groups in society. As forms of mass communication are directed at us, in large part through the spaces of the home, we are now more cognizant that this can be experienced as both overbearing and an intrusion on self-expression. These concerns are more pertinent under conditions in which communication technologies have become deeply insinuated in our lives. The home is thus a multifaceted space and a site of complex tensions that produce it as a deeply *social* space, despite our feelings that this is "our" space and that it is a place of self-expression and idiosyncrasy.

This is a book that foregrounds the often entangled connections linking the physical dwellings we inhabit for basic survival (the house and its varying forms as flats, apartments, single-family homes, terraces, bungalows, etc.), the way that social relationships inhabit and generate emotional bonds to those spaces (the idea of our home), and the social and economic forces that shape these buildings and our lives more generally. These are important distinctions that form the basis of what we elucidate here. One of the first things to say about a house is that it is a key physical but also social space in which we develop as individuals (Winnicott, 1965). It is from our home above all that we emerge everyday as individual social actors who form part of the societies on which anthropologists, sociologists, and other social scientists focus. In this sense, it is surprising that there have been relatively few attempts by sociologists to speak coherently about houses, homes, and societies, despite their profound importance to the lives of individuals and the wider collectivities of social life. Many of the major contributions to Western sociology came about as a result of observations concerning societal change as a result of growing urbanization (Park and Burgess, 1925/1967), yet this did not often translate into deeper analyses of domestic life, its interior problems and processes, the provision or lack of housing, and so on, despite these being massive issues Western nations faced in the late nineteenth and early twentieth centuries. We might characterize this lacuna in terms of the development of social science as places and people taking precedence over domestic spaces. Many problems analyzed by early, domestically focused research pioneers (such as Seebohm Rowntree in the United Kingdom and Jane Addams in the United States, who examined the lack of amenities and utilities, poverty, and appalling material conditions) have diminished in the West, though we will return to the processes of exclusion and poverty in the West and beyond throughout the book. In the past half-century, these problems are now found in shocking abundance in the Global South (Satterthwaite and Mitlin, 2013), particularly alongside accelerating urbanization. We will be considering these questions of theory, problems of identity, and the empirical reality of many of these problems across this book.

We can begin with a simple mental exercise in which we consider the image of a house in our mind's eye. Invariably, we think of a structure with four windows (probably quartered) and a door—a square house with a peaked roof and a chimney (with or without smoke). This suggests something about the power of shared ideas, social values, and our impressions of the home that is preferred and which we aspire to own. These viewpoints also tell us about the subtle yet very deep influence of society and the groups we circulate among that shape our ideas and desires. Where do we feel these impressions and ideas come from? Do we simply choose these ideal forms on our own, or are they brought to us through our upbringing and socialization? Thinking about these questions sets the stage for revealing a central, thematic question in this book: What do we know about the relationship between us as more or less free individuals, in households of varying permutations (singles, lone parents, nuclear families, extended kin groups, shared homes in multiple occupation, gay households, people made homeless who are temporarily sleeping on a friend's sofa, overcrowded families with three kids in a small bedroom) in houses and dwellings of almost endless varieties and configurations? Despite the complexity of these relationships, we know that various forms of expression and consumption repeat and map with other forms of social division, often based on varying levels of wealth and resource. Even if we want such a home, do we have the ability to afford it? This book is all about such relationships, connections, habits, and expressions in which our home, the dwelling we feel a sense of attachment to, is reconsidered.

More on what the terrain of sociology of housing involves will be presented in due course. For now, let us ponder why the idea of the single-family home permeates our subconscious so pervasively. We know that this type of ideal home accommodates 23% of households in the United Kingdom (UK 2011 census data), 60% in the United States (this ranges from 72% in rural Kansas down to 42% in New York state [US 2010 census data]), to a staggering 79% in Australia (the city of Perth is even higher, at 84% [ABS, 2012]). These statistics supply important information about the look, feel, culture, and nature of the domestic built environment in these three societies and quite literally how people live there. Such comparisons highlight that our ambitions and opportunities are enormously influenced by where we live (urban or rural; wealthy or poorer country), how housing is produced, and by whom. We will begin to dig into these issues in more detail as we progress; for now, let's pause and consider what the language of the single-family dwelling reveals about our housing system (its production, layout, consumption, and fit within broader towns and cities) and prevailing social values—about the aspirations and desires of many.

It should be evident from our opening discussion that the ideas and values we may share or indeed feel to be our very own are not simply innate impulses, but are shaped by social conditions, economic conditions, and the way that human society is both organized and divided. Even if we dig just a little, we begin to find that our preconceptions and assured positions are quickly eroded—homes vary in shape, size, and function; household units are culturally varied; and these variations shift over time alongside social changes (such as prevailing attitudes to separation or rising wealth which may have negative or positive impact on whether or how much individuals can realize their housing

ambitions). Homes are owned, invested in, borrowed against, sold, and rented. In all of this, we must fundamentally recognize that personal experiences of bricks and mortar are intense and critical to our lives and happiness and also that these outcomes are shaped by deep social, economic, and political forces that affect the experiences of individuals and groups within societies. Thus, we find that minority ethnic households are more likely to be owners in the United Kingdom because of prejudice from landlords (Arbaci, 2007); that young people are more likely to rent because they are less likely to have sufficient resources; that society often fails to accommodate all people; and that family violence, breakdown, and sudden personal tragedy generate homelessness. To view this variability of human outcomes and problems as natural or inevitable is a misdiagnosis; instead, we must provide critical analyses of how social inequalities, government policies, economic systems, social class identities and resources, ethnicity, and culture combine to profoundly influence the housing problems and phenomena we see around us.

Introducing the core concepts: House, home, household, tenure

Much of this book rests extensively on some core concepts that require brief explanation in order for many of the arguments, ideas, and research presented here to make sense. The study of housing requires us not only to be attentive and discerning to detail but also to notice connections that have wider societal significance. We should also be rigorous and reflexive in our research by maintaining a critical stance when interrogating the language and ideas of lawyers, economists, social policy analysts, geographers, and other social scientists to consider how housing and homes are produced, consumed, experienced, accessed, and lost. We begin by providing an introduction to some of the key terms that we will be using throughout the book.

A **house** is a domestic dwelling, a structure in which people live. It is where one or more households (see below) live on a more or less permanent basis. To talk of houses is to consider the nature of dwellings, physical structures designed for human habitation and which protect their inhabitants from the elements and from dangers (animals or other human predators). Across different nation-states, the range and form of these structures are immense (Oliver, 2003), reflecting vernacular styles, the ready availability of particular materials, and the structures of society and needs generated by cultural norms. Thus, we see the "balloon" wood frames of US Midwest homes in the early twentieth century, the brick-built semi of British suburbia, the Indian single-story bungalow that so influenced suburban development globally, and the detached Australian homestead built rapidly using timber and corrugated-steel roofs. As we later discuss, these variations in structure and internal design shape our lives in deep yet subtle ways; the small kitchens of New York apartments generate regular forays to cheap diners; the increasing subdivision of private bedroom spaces allowed partners new privacy from children who historically shared the same room; and front rooms or lounges provided new spaces for conscious display and the expression of personal taste (Bryson, 2010).

The functions of a house

Shelter from elements
Protection of the household within—from animals or intruders
Display of standing within a community of society
Source of pride, satisfaction
A space to be ourselves, free from surveillance or control
Physical space required to enable social reproduction, allowing
    family units to continue and thrive
A means of offering a space of physical and mental security
Maintenance of the economic unit of the household
A space for familial and sexual relations
A building block of broader social and economic systems

(Adapted from Loewy and Snaith, 1967)

The idea contained in the word **domestic** refers to a sense of space that is calm, private, and protected, a space that in many ways nurtures. The root of the word comes from the Latin word *domus*, used to refer to a house. This root is also interesting because it is from this that we form words like *domain*, which are also used to express a sense of territory and control—the home is the space over which we have power and authority and on which a wide range of legal entitlements are conferred, not least the right to expel any intruder and historically a space in which the head of the household (almost invariably a male figure, even if a matriarch managed and maintained the house and its members) had many rights to control those inside (Gillis and Hollows, 2008).

If a house is the physical dwelling, then **home** refers to the deeper emotional bonds and attachments we feel in relation to a particular house, sometimes more than one. For Blunt and Dowling, the home is a kind of "a spatial imaginary: a set of intersecting and variable ideas and feelings, which are related to context, and which construct places, extend across spaces and scales, and connect places" (2006: 2). The home is usually the place we return to each day, but this belies real difficulties and complexities in practice. If you have moved across national boundaries, do you think of home as the house, city, or nation you come from? If you have a second home, is the home that you spend less time in the place you really call home (Paris, 2008)? As a student, is your home your student lodgings or hall, or is it where your parents live now? Such questions show that including the subjective experiences and affiliations that people have toward bricks and mortar, timber and steel, is an important component in sociological conceptions of the house and home. Additionally, much can and should be discussed in relation to the problems and traumas that many face inside the home itself. What happens when we try to capture the fraught and traumatized world of the victims of domestic abuse who have homes but whose emotional response to these particular places may be one of terror and conflict (these themes are revisited in Chapter 5)? These examples show that we need to be flexible when attempting to conceptualize and understand social phenomena; we clearly need basic definitions, but we must see how the complexities of social life as it is lived bring difficulties, but also enlightening examples that tell us more about how life is lived. More than anything else, the idea of the home is critical in enabling a refined sociological imagination that addresses the complex linkages between this affective zone and the wider society to which we are connected via its protective capacities. Although we would not deploy the term *sociospatial system* to encapsulate "home" Saunders and Williams, in their article "The Constitution of the Home: Towards a Research Agenda," make clear the interconnections that weave through all aspects of social life,

> Our society is not atomised, but is structured through a variety of household types. Few men, women or children are islands, for it is through their membership of household units that they are integrated in one way or another into the wider complex of social institutions which comprise their society.... The home, in other words, is a sociospatial system. It is not reducible either to the social unit of the household or to the physical unit of the house, for it is the active

and reproduced fusion of the two. The home is the most basic and simple of modern socio-spatial systems. Functionally (i.e. in terms of both its social and spatial organisation) it is indivisible. (1988: 82–3)

The term *household* refers to the complex range of social structures contained within a particular dwelling or house, which are also subject to change over time. Yet what is meant by *household* varies to some extent between societies and cultures. The ideal or typical household is commonly imagined as a family consisting of parents and children, but this belies the reality of diverse and complex kinds of social clusters within homes. A household may be more or less those who consider themselves to be living together, so this is clearly not as simple as referring to a family. As students, you probably do not think of yourselves as a family in the house or flat you occupy (unless you are studying from home and are still within your family setting); however, you may or may not be a household. If we use the definition used in the US census (all the people who occupy a housing unit), you are indeed a household in one dwelling (the same is the case in the United Kingdom, where a household is defined as "one person living alone or a group of people [not necessarily related] living at the same address with common housekeeping—that is, sharing either a living room or sitting room or at least one meal a day"), but whether you *feel* like a household may be a different issue entirely. As we will see, the variability of households is immense: singles, couples, families of various kinds and sizes, intergenerational families, and mixes of genders and sexualities; it may include combinations of legal bonds like marriage or involve the complexities of separation and transition between parental homes, and in all of this, takes into account the incredible array of feelings and experiences that we undergo as a result of moving through these types of social groups and changes to our housing situations. In short, qualitative insights like these show us that attempts to impose rigid classifications are fraught with difficulty.

It is important to understand how changes in our household situation relate to our life course and to physical structures of houses. We may start in a family (which may take various forms) in a home, in the care of the state, or we may be destitute in a zone of conflict or natural disaster. We may leave home to get a job or, more often, after some time working as we save to access homes of our own. We often shift from being the dependent child to renting a flat or small house, and we may feel both lucky and burdened at some point if we start to purchase a home using money borrowed from banks, mutual societies, or through the financial gifts of our parents. These shifting patterns, often termed **housing pathways** or **housing careers** (Clapham, 2002), refer to these transitions and reflect the attempts of sociologists to understand not only these trajectories but also variations in our social outcomes, housing problems, and deeper material inequalities that run through societies. These changes can be revealed by considering where we hope to go in life, whether we have a stable job (now less and less often a possibility), and whether we must borrow to buy the kind of home from which to start, perhaps an inner city apartment with a professional job in the same city. The idea of starting on a housing ladder, an ever increasing sense of material wealth achieved by buying and selling houses; changing our household position, possibly to a family with children (increasing levels of household/family breakdown also applies pressure on the housing system); and so on, represent a kind of deep ideal or imagined typical life path for many people. Not only does the reality differ from this ladder or pathway, but it reflects the kind of heteronormative and materialistic bases of our societies and economies, which are now closely connected to the fortunes and desires of the home-owning population (we will deal much more with the politics and economics of home ownership in Chapter 7). Indeed, one of the shifts that we will chart later is the ambivalence toward ownership by new generations of young people exposed to the increasing precariousness of the labor market or trapped in parental homes or rented accommodation.

Any discussion of owning and renting and their respective merits and downsides brings us to the concept of **tenure**. Housing tenure essentially refers to the legal claim we have to a particular dwelling and thereby relates to the conditions of our occupancy and the rights we have to stay in such a place. But it can also be thought of as a set of institutional arrangements and social practices (Ruonavaara, 1993). Housing tenure can be split broadly into renting and owning, but again the issue is complex. We can be called homeowners if we own homes outright (around 34% of US and 32% of UK households, see Jones and Richardson, 2014) or if we are paying off a home loan (usually for around 20–25 years). Although rates of ownership across the globe vary significantly, it is generally accepted that the aspiration to own runs high and has become normalized in social discourses focused on the essential desirability and economic benefits of possession, and even the idea that humans have an innate preference toward home ownership (Saunders, 1990). As sociologists, we must look to comparative global data, at particular national and political systems, the regulation of construction, and the different crucial sectors like public renting, as well as variations between these, to understand more about the realities of how the desirability of tenure is fundamentally shaped by economic realities and our social position. To offer one example, many people in the United Kingdom prefer to own in order to escape the poor quality of the private rented sector and so as not to waste money on rent, but instead to store wealth in a property. In some European countries, government regulations give tenants rights for certain quality standards and restrict sudden rises in rents or possible eviction. In these countries, renters are able to exercise more choice and suffer from lower insecurity than renters experience in the United States and Australia, where there is much less government intervention. Yet it remains the case that the tenure structure of the United Kingdom, the United States, and Australia (Ireland, Greece, and Spain also) shows them to be "homeowner societies" despite new complexities around many people both renting and owning at the same time (Hulse and Mcpherson, 2014). The term is not used to mean that most people own their own homes, but rather that such socio*tenurial* structures have important implications for social structures more generally in terms of inequalities and opportunities and the kind of political-economic contexts they nest within.

As writers like Forrest and Murie (1988) observed, social norms that focus on how we consume homes are reinforced by government policies and economic systems that privilege owning by making it more desirable and potentially more profitable (Hamnett, 2005). Keeping interest rates low to make mortgages cheap and the ongoing withdrawal of welfare entitlements in many Western countries has also made buying a home important as a source of investment and protection in old age, often termed "asset-based welfare" (the hope that paying down a mortgage or successive buying and selling of homes will bring its own returns). So embedded have these conditions become that many housing analysts view home ownership as performing as an ideology, a prevailing normative order supported by governments and ruling economic and political agencies (house builders, political parties seeking electoral support, and financial institutions seeking to sell mortgage products and related insurances) that again penetrates our mental frames of reference and guides our social actions (Ronald, 2007). We may feel that we simply want to own our own home, but more social reflection is required: we need to know how these preferences are informed by social norms and aspirations, key actors, institutions, and economic incentives. We will continue to reflect on these ideas and debates throughout the book.

Although the technical definition of *home ownership* varies in different nation-states, renting can be broadly divided into two types: public and private renting. Public housing, either directly owned by the state or municipal organizations, including cities and local authorities, or by non-profit, state-supported landlords like housing associations (more on this later), has become deeply stigmatized (Hastings and Dean, 2003; Atkinson and Jacobs, 2010). Private rented housing, offered by land-lords who may be individual or institutional landlords is second type. The respective size of these tenures is shown in Table 1.1. As we show later, the size of each of these sectors is often seen as critical to how

Table 1.1 Percentage of households in key housing tenures, for selected countries.

	Percent Owner Occupied
Romania	96
Poland	84
Norway	83
Spain	78
Iceland	78
Greece	76
Portugal	74
Finland	74
Italy	73
Australia	**73**
Ireland	70
Sweden	70
Netherlands	67
United States	**65**
United Kingdom	**65**
France	64
Denmark	63
Austria	57
Germany	53

Sources: Australia 2011 census, by population; US American Housing Survey Data, 2013; Eurostat 2015, by population; UK 2011 census data, by household.

individuals feel they are doing in life, how well politicians feel the econ-omy is doing (rising house prices and sales are often seen as intrinsically good) and, more problematically, have been implicated in the massive ongoing financial crisis experienced globally (because it was the resale of bad mortgage debts that brought the collapse of US banks that were unwittingly exposed to the risks of nonpayment by low-income own-ers, as described in Chapter 6). Tenure also matters to us critically as individuals, in terms of the decisions that households have to make about where to move (homes need to be available to buy or to rent to us and at a cost we can afford to bear) and what tenure will help people realize their long-term ambitions for security in life. This means that many people have become pundit economists, tracking changes in interest rates, looking at new house-building projects, or monitoring house-price websites to discover new opportunities for capital gain in a system that is stressed in many cities and regions globally.

Conclusion

In this brief introduction, we have set out the key terrain of a housing sociology and its primary concerns. We have suggested that these core interests lie in the production of a critical and structured understanding of the experience of the home and its production, as well as the range of key actors and institutions involved in these experiences. A sociol-ogy of housing thus has very broad concerns that connect individuals to the physical structures of their homes while seeing these domestic "units" as lived experiences and daily life that is shaped by larger social structures, forces, and divisions. In this sense, what appears to us within our personal experience is a social space that is shaped by the actions of governments, builders, social taste, class differences, and inequalities in income and wealth (which affect our relative exposure to housing problems or the kind of home we can afford).

In addition, questions of gender, disability, and other key influences on social life are played out through the life of the home and indeed may be reproduced or reinforced by the social forces and cultures that inhabit institutions within and beyond the home. This can be seen in the way that housing wealth is inherited, thus offering the rich a means to produce new generations or have a head start in life and who also seek to benefit their future generations. The continued inability of many societies to tackle significant housing problems (notably, quality and affordability) marks out even the most "advanced" or wealthy nations.

As we will see in this book, housing problems are a mainstay of sociological analysis but are less often recognized as such—the sociological curriculum, if we may call it that, rarely reflects the primacy and relevance of housing to contemporary society and the global economy in which massive international and regional inequalities fuel flows of international migration that intersect with questions of climate change and low-intensity warfare. Social forces, economics and cultural structures play a significant role in shaping the experience of daily household life, our access to opportunities, the potential impacts of our housing on our and our children's health and the kinds of neighborhoods and city contexts we live in. These relationships place housing, systems of housing provision, regulatory frameworks, and social categories and divisions at the forefront of sociology in its attempt to understand, explain, and connect to efforts at doing something about such problems.

2 Theoretical Perspectives on Housing

Introduction

In the opening chapter, we introduced key terms and concepts that are deployed to understand housing and the home. We also made the point that housing is not only a broad field of study but also a critical area for social investigation, given its massive importance to individuals, social groups, governments, and supporting industries (builders, decorators, home furnishings companies, and so on) and the formation of deep-running social norms and discourses. As individuals and members of a range of social groups, we are products of this complex amalgam of forces, and this has generated concerted efforts by social researchers to develop increasingly sophisticated theoretical frameworks to understand housing problems, how housing systems work, and how important the politics of housing is to the satisfaction of human need (Dorling, 2014). In this chapter, our focus turns to the development of housing studies in sociology and aligned disciplines such as human geography and politics, to show the advances that have been made in understanding housing and to highlight key developments in this field of inquiry.

Despite what we have said so far about the importance and place of housing in social life, it is important to recognize that housing is an under-studied and under-theorized area of sociological investigation. However, to consider housing as a deeply embedded aspect of social experience, as the central mediating point of many or indeed most of our social experience, it is important to recognize the home as both a critical and exciting area of study. Through the study of housing, we can see how complex systems (economic, political, and social) affect the lives of all of us and the degree to which we are able to live happy, healthy, and fulfilled lives. Perhaps more importantly, sociologists are drawn to consider housing because it is so integral to the maintenance of the human body and the social relationships and support systems that maintain it (Highmore, 2014). Even a brief glance at the lack of housing in many African or Latin American cities, the rise of giant slums of informal dwellings, and the immense variations in housing quality and outcomes in the Global West show that many of the most massive human problems are in fact also housing problems—whether this be in terms of how we may access housing, its variable quality or cost (which thereby affects a wide range of secondary domains of social life), loss, or absence (Lemanski, 2011). Such problems are both issues in their own right, but more broadly, true to the concerns of sociologists, they signal the presence of deeper social divides and fissures connected to social class and inequalities of access and provision as well as key factors like gender, sexuality, age, and so on.

The home is somewhere most people live (because it is essential we acknowledge the presence of those who suffer various forms of homelessness) and the place that we begin our "training," or socialization, into the wider patterns and structure of society around us. The household or family is where we are nurtured and prepare to join the society at large. But this apparently universal narrative has to be dissected because the project of a critical sociology is to think about and identify the underlying variability of social life and the deeper problems around us. Home is often unstable and potentially a source of danger (see Chapter 6) or a space of varying household formations that may diverge from the ordinary, the typical, or the socially normalized. For housing sociologists, these problems and variations are essential aspects of study; around the world, many millions of people do not live with the assurance of home (Davis, 2006). They live in flimsy and insecure homes with poor or nonexistent services and essential infrastructure, including around 39% of the world's population without access to adequate sanitation (World Health Organization and UNICEF, 2006). For millions of others, warfare, low-level conflict, and climate change have forced people from their homes, to try to find new homes and temporary accommodations that may be hostile. Even in the richest societies, the problem of homelessness remains an acute housing priority. In this context, a sociology of housing needs to understand not only cultures but also material problems. The sociology of housing is therefore the study of the relationship between society and the individual as this is mediated by the home, with reference to a range of social, economic, and political forces. In short, we can describe the sociology of housing as an attempt to understand and critique the following:

1. the social influences on the provision of dwellings and experience of home;
2. the socioeconomic effects of housing systems and the impact of housing tenure (whether we are owners or renters from the state or private landlords);
3. modes of governance, personal welfare, and structures of the economy more broadly.

More specifically, the sociology of housing relates to the following needs:

- to provide a theoretically and empirically informed understanding of the role of the home in its various social, physical, and subjective aspects;
- develop understandings of the position of the home within economic, political, social, and cultural systems;
- pursue a questioning outlook regarding the mediation of social inequalities and gender roles via housing tenure and wealth;
- connect the "building block" of the domestic dwelling to wider theoretical accounts of society given in classical and contemporary accounts;
- unsettle and raise questions around our emancipation and maturation in relation to domestic spaces; and
- generate insights into the nature of home in an international context and to the social and political projects of nation-states and localities.

No single theorist or body of theory has provided a substantive engagement with housing. Many of the earliest statements relating to a coherent housing sociology came from American sociologists in the immediate postwar period. Writing in 1947, the Chicago sociologist Louis Wirth (generally credited with major works on social ecology and crime in the city) wrote for the *American Sociological Review* on "Housing as a Field of Sociological Research" (Wirth, 1947). Wirth argued that such a project could be characterized by three key areas of investigation. The first is the question of social values and considered preferences for design, style, size, and architecture as well as what was needed from the home in general terms. Second, for Wirth, housing expressed deeper social values through such preferences, but he also emphasized the need to recognize how individual homes are located within neighborhoods, communities, and cities, which we must also be aware of and understand as systems that influence how we live in our own homes. Finally, Wirth argued that a sociology of housing should be interested in issues of social change and the role of government in tackling a range of housing problems through social policies. This might take the form of interest in the kind of building regulations governing standards, the capacity of industry to build sufficient homes (it is important to remember that he was writing at a time of real anxiety about there not being enough housing resources in the immediate postwar period, an issue shared by many countries at this time, which echoes many problems we see around us today) and the role of government in these issues. Wirth's ideas therefore suggested an expansive role for sociologists for the years ahead.

Soon after Wirth, the noted social theorist Robert Merton wrote an essay in 1948 (see also Merton, West, Jahoda, and Selvin, 1951) titled *Social policy and social research in Housing in the references*. This connected housing to a wide range of social factors, but with a particular focus on the emerging pressures on individuals and households who were increasingly living at that time in the kind of planned settlements that had been devised by governments as a response to housing shortages and slum conditions (more on the role of the state in Chapter 8). For Merton, links could be found between the physical qualities of housing and a range of "social morbidities" that included crime and poverty. As we will see later, the interest of sociologists in these conditions is part of a broader story about a range of interventions by governments, spurred by impressions derived from research that bad housing leads to poor social outcomes of various kinds. Merton was also interested in how the question of what is built, and for whom, was shaped by powerful social interests—in other words, housing researchers were part of a broader politics around housing provision and a series of contested interests. Researchers were often the poorer cousins of powerful vested interests, both in government and in the house-building industry. As we see later, the question of regulatory standards was a key element of these contests, with each of these groups seeking to maximize the benefits to the occupants of housing or to the profit-driven concerns of builders to offer cheap housing, which was also popular with lower-income households. Merton also acknowledged the need to apply social theory to social problems like housing and the need to understand more deeply how, as individuals, we are also linked to neighborhoods and to society via the homes we inhabit. As Merton commented, the new kinds of housing and community formation in the United States at that time were a ripe opportunity for sociologists to consider:

> In the continued growth in planned communities and large-scale housing developments, as distinct from the accretion of individual

units within and around pre-existing neighbourhoods, contemporary housing provides an unparalleled near-experimental setting for the study of "what might be" rather than the continued observation of "what is" and "what has been" in human relations within the local community. (1951: 185–6)

Merton's agenda was echoed in a later statement about the content of a sociology of housing offered by Donald Foley (1980). Foley argued that sociology alone was not enough to understand the wider range of problems associated with housing. Like much social research today, Foley argued that work across disciplines, particularly sociology and social policy, was essential to understanding housing. This raises some quandaries regarding the terrain of a housing "sociology" and for sociology itself because it is clear that to provide an effective and insightful account of the range of human experience, systems of production, and consumption and problems, it is essential to include concepts and techniques of other disciplines—including human geography, social policy, political science, economics, and planning—that address housing issues. This is an exciting challenge rather than some kind of insurmountable obstacle: to be good sociologists, we must develop forms of expertise that engage diverse modes of social investigation, and move away from our comfort zones as sociologists. This point is highlighted in Foley's essay, where he connects deprivation in housing (lack of quality, availability, the low income of some tenants, as examples) and how these factors come to affect other key dimensions of life and opportunity. Of course these considerations are the meat and drink of sociological inquiry. Therefore, a sociology of housing should aim to understand how the home and the household and its material conditions come to shape outcomes in the fields of education, health, status, jobs, markets and so on. Similarly, Foley argued that housing conditions could also be linked to community "development"—where we live and how housing is planned have impacts on how we experience our environment and each other as well as other social groups—differentiated by class and ethnicity but also by divisions around taste, levels of housing consumption tenure and the social character of neighborhood. These factors remain core concerns for planners and housing providers today and continue to influence the move from housing "estates" to "scattered sites" in the United States, and housing policies that aimed to create more social mix in local areas (see Chapter 9).

The link between home, safety, and predictability: Ontological security

One major area of consideration for sociologists in relation to housing has been the development of the concept of ontological security. This refers to the human need for assurances in the predictability of daily social life and our deep need for a sense that the world around us is stable and can offer a sense of continuity. This idea was initially developed by Giddens (1991), who argued that this was an important consideration in trying to understand the deeper psychological foundations of individuals situated within wider social structures and processes. Again, there are echoes here of Merton's move to consider the psychic impact of particular kinds of housing, notably the density of planned communities built by public administrations. But for many housing theorists, the idea of ontological security has enabled a conceptualization of the individual and the household within wider patterns of sociotenurial structure. In other words, for some researchers, the relative security of the worldview of individuals might be improved where this tenure offered a sense of escape from private landlordism, personal autonomy, and the ability to control, modify, and tend the space of the home.

Summary of some of the claims advanced for home ownership as a preferable tenure:

- Expression of the need for permanent and controllable space
- Intrusion and control of capitalism in the sphere of work and production, countered by a private sphere of control and escape
- A sense of freedom and autonomy
- Financial security—a means to make money and a store of value (equity) over time
- Freedom from intrusion or exploitation by private landlords

---

These ideas were most strongly expressed in Peter Saunders's ambitious work *A Nation of Homeowners* (1990). Saunders asserted, without any empirical evidence, that owning is an innate human preference precisely because of the way that this tenure might be more able to respond to the deep emotional and psychological needs of individuals. Although we can clearly see that many people want to own their own homes, we have also seen periods in history when the repossession of homes (see Chapter 5) became mass social phenomena. The ownership of homes can also be erased or seized within the context of war, by the construction of megaprojects, or by the massive consequences of ecological catastrophe and climate change. Although we can understand how home ownership may be satisfying and create a sense of perpetuity and control, we also need to offer a critical assessment of the idea that feelings and attachment are natural within a social context; as social animals, we are permeated by rules and norms, ideals, aspirations, and goals generated within our societies and that fundamentally affect the economic, social, and political manner in which particular tenures are seen as more or less desirable, secure, or achievable. Despite such critiques, we should also understand how some of the major themes found in global sociology, such as the socially strained relations and fragmentation of societies, and social trajectories described by major social theorists like Beck (1992) or Lipovetsky and Charles (2005), suggest a rising desirability to own a home as a means of offering a space of relative control and emancipation from anxiety, as well as a means of potential financial security. Despite the risks attached to ownership, such as repossession (Ford, Burrows, and Nettleton, 2001), there is an even greater need of social subjects to seek ways, no matter how illusory or temporary, to engender a sense of security and foundation in their daily lives. And despite this view, we may usefully reflect back on the political economy of housing provision that continues to reflect the social values of private wealth appreciation and personal freedom that are so often aligned with the idea of owning one's home, as Kemeny argued in *The Great Australian Nightmare*:

> The homeownership ideology is by now deeply entrenched in the housing folklore, as well as in the housing policies of most capitalist societies. Indeed, so much is this so that there is very little likelihood that tenure-neutral housing policies will ever replace the current homeownership policies in most countries, at least in the near future. (1983: 275)

Many governments have connected economic growth, electoral success, and home ownership (Dorling, 2014). Dupuis and Thorns (1996) have used these ideas in their analysis of ontological security as a way of framing a series of interviews with homeowners in New Zealand. In this work, they found that home ownership was frequently seen as an insurance against the economic risks of retirement. The need to provide for oneself (a very strong value in the "frontier capitalist" societies of the United States, Australia, and New Zealand) is an important aspect of these feelings, found in a country with a long, deep collective social memory that rubs through the wider culture of New Zealand society. Fears of a return of a major economic depression fuelled the desire to be homeowners so they could look after themselves. Today many states have cut back major elements of welfare provision, advancing the very real need to find provision, and this has even further amplified the sense that paying off one's mortgage and increases in house values can be used to develop the resources needed to pay for retirement and offer a more secured mindset throughout life. The ownership of a home and getting on the ladder offer a means of finding a more secure sense of one's place in the world, to say nothing of the need many people have to fit in with widely held social values that place the home and home ownership at the center of social life.

Housing studies

The contemporary study of housing is a discrete area of social research that operates across the boundaries of a number of disciplines. It involves sociologists, geographers, and political scientists who define themselves less by their discipline and more by their object of study. Academic journals have been critical for creating and maintaining the field of housing studies, particularly *Housing, Theory and Society* and *Housing Studies* (which has operated since 1986). The work of Kemeny (1992) has been instrumental in helping such research to be more theoretically developed and critical, politically. Yet a number of risks have been associated with the rise of housing studies as a discrete area of research and theorization. Atkinson and Jacobs (2009) have used the work of Kemeny to argue that it has been driven by the agendas of policy makers and governments (themselves in thrall to the private interests of prospective and existing homeowners and the building industry), given that it has been a more applied area of social investigation concerned with how particular social problems might be tackled. This accusation is often recognized by contract researchers working in consultancies and universities, who are often caught on short-term project funding and the need to find continuing work. Allen and Imrie (2010) have provided a sociological analysis of these conditions and the way in which job insecurity in universities with neoliberal administrations and declining government funding have tended to produce compliant and uncritical research. Such accusations are well made and understood by some researchers who find their more critical views and ideas muffled by this kind of work environment. Of course, the second key problem, Kemeny's accusation that housing studies were conceptually unfocused, proceeds in large part from these problems. In *Housing and Social Theory* (1992), Kemeny argued that the general absence of housing as an element of sociological theorizing led the field toward the production of empiricist accounts that provided description without sufficient attempts at providing deeper, more explanatory frameworks. The danger for Kemeny was a sociology of housing that was largely incapable of providing sufficiently rich insights into the meaning and position of housing. Housing researchers subject to short time frames were inclined toward a kind of "epistemic drift" and failed to engage critically with the question of what constituted robust knowledge of housing problems because of an attachment to dealing with the needs of research policy clients. Kemeny argued that housing researchers were led into producing largely descriptive, rather than critical, forms of scholarship under the pressure of policy makers to produce publications that respond and legitimize the day-to-day concerns of government agencies.

Kemeny's critique has contemporary resonance because the context of housing has altered quite dramatically over the last 20 years. As we will discuss later in the book, the most discernible changes include the residualization of social housing stock, globalization processes that have weakened the capacity of national governments to manage their economy, and speculative investment in housing that has led to home ownership priced beyond the means of aspiring, first-time buyers and rents that are now unaffordable for even middle-income wage earners.

In this context, it is incumbent on all students with an interest in understanding housing to choose the appropriate theoretical frameworks for investigation and also to avoid what Wright Mills (1959) termed "abstracted empiricism"—in other words, a reliance and retreat into data without connecting this to social conditions and explanatory frameworks that offer more comprehensive ways of understanding the social world. Mills particularly had in mind the tendency of some researchers to limit their inquiries to the mere collection and classification of data, rather than engaging in critique. These concerns remain relevant for housing researchers today, when much research remains lost in descriptive statistics, with deeper thinking often absent from the process.

In this chapter, we identify some of the key theoretical perspectives that have been successfully applied within the particular field of housing research. The two most influential approaches are what can be termed *structuralist* and *interpretevist*. Structural explanations of housing focus on the mechanisms that underpin the phenomena we can observe. The most widely used structural theories applied to housing are Marxism and related post-Marxist frameworks (such as Harvey, 1973, 2009; or Gough, Eisenschitz, and McCulloch, 2006) that operate using many of Marx's ideas about the nature of capitalist economies and the workings of the broader economy. Among the key concepts deployed by structural theories is the idea of capital as a form of value and social class. For Marxists, housing outcomes and problems are the outcome of inequities in the distribution of wealth and power. Under such conditions, the task of housing research and scholarship is to bring to the fore the causes of inequity, show how governments very often serve the interests of the well-off at the expense of the poor, and locate the nexus of agency within social formations.

The second theoretical perspective that has been influential is the Weberian approach to housing. The orientation of Weber is toward the capacity of individuals and agencies to shape outcomes. Research investigations that draw upon Weberian concepts have tended to focus attention on the practices and individual actors. Researchers are now generally cognizant of these issues and are adept at drawing upon broader sociological theory to advance their analyses. Within the corpus of housing studies, some research has sought to make use of *inter alia* Foucauldian theories of governmentality that explicitly focus on the way in which power is exercised and the role played by ideology (McKee, 2009) and Pierre Bourdieu's concept of habitus (used to consider the ways that class identities are maintained through social practices over time). More on Bourdieu in Chapter 9, but at this juncture we note his influence for scholars seeking to understand experiences of home (Easthope, 2004). Some mention of Beck's notion of risk society (2009) is also apposite here. For Beck, risk has become a defining aspect of the contemporary era as individuals seek to negotiate the changing and uncertain aspects of their lives. Scholars such as Beck (2009) have used the concept of risk to consider how individuals make sense of their housing choices (Croft, 2001; Beck, 2009). Recent research no longer situates the home as a backdrop or setting for more tangible practices, but as a worthy object of study in its own right and within these important social contexts and understandings of how society operates today.

Housing scholars grapple with another important tension that straddles analysis and prescription—whether analysts of housing should be descriptive or make normative assertions about what should be done to improve conditions and reduce inequalities. On the one hand, the primary task of scholarship is seen by some as simply to understand housing and its context; and on the other, some scholars see their primary task as one of "speaking truth to power," that is pointing out the defects of current arrangements, and see research as a basis for reform. In this book, we have aimed to reconcile this tension by seeking to provide insights that are relevant to practice, theoretically informed but also, when needed, critical of government agencies.

Academics often seek to refine and improve the conceptual vocabulary for their investigations, making additions and changes to language and underlying ideas used to describe critical issues around them. In the context of housing, core concepts such as gender, class, the state, market, and tenure continue to be subject to interrogation. Often this interrogation consists of refining and critiquing concepts and determining the best methods to further understanding. We would suggest that today there is a general acceptance among scholars that the key tasks for investigation should encompass the role of government, understanding the relative efficacy of markets, the taxation system, the meaning of home, and the role of neoliberal ideology and its influence on the conduct of policy making. Understanding the mechanisms, structures, and workings of these forces and institutions remains contested, and for good reason. To understand, analyze, and make suggestions for the improvement of housing conditions, we are compelled to enter political debates and tread a difficult path in offering critical understandings that often dig beneath and subvert superficial layers of commonly accepted understandings. A good example of this is in the area of housing markets, where academics—to say nothing of politicians and policy makers in governments—may have very different ideas about how markets work, how they link to the role of governments and political parties, and whether and to what extent they address key areas of housing need. Many academic researchers have found that systematic analysis has tended to generate ideas that are often unsympathetic toward mainstream government and pro-market ideas (Allen, 2005).

Our discussion up to now has focused on the concepts that can be deployed to further analysis, but some consideration is required of the theories of knowledge underpinning housing research to understand the type of enquiries undertaken. By this, we mean questions of epistemology, the concern with what counts for knowledge, and how we come by that knowledge. We can note that positivism, the idea that social science can and should be essentially an enterprise based on a model of inquiry that assumes the world is fully measurable, knowable, and predictable, has sustained extensive critique. Put simply, it presupposes that there is an objective external world amenable to measurement by social scientists, and sound conclusions can be drawn from these forms of investigation. The most influential approach that counters the assumptions implicit within positivist informed housing studies is usually termed *interpretivism* or *constructivism*. In contrast to positivism, constructivism attempts to ascertain the *verstehen* (understanding) held by individuals and their motives. Those who draw from a constructionist epistemology tend to rely on qualitative methods when collecting data, such as interviews and participatory observation. Constructionist-informed investigations have been especially influential in areas such as homelessness (Fitzpatrick, 2005) and the experience of the home (Somerville, 1997). In policy analysis, constructionist research has also sought to understand the competing claims of interest groups and how they exert influence (Marston, 2004; Lund, 2011).

Another theoretical approach referred to as Actor Network Theory (ANT), based on the writings of Michel Callon (1986), Bruno Latour (1991), and John Law (1992), has been influential among scholars exploring the connections between agents. A key claim of ANT is that both human and material objects generate effects, so the task of research extends beyond societal relationships (see Shove, Watson, Hand, and Ingram, 2007; Murdoch, 1998). In other words, material objects perform not in the same way as human agents, yet they may still have agency to the extent that they affect the world around them and social actors (see Thrift, 2007). The most obvious examples are doors and keys, chairs and tables, and TVs—all of which generate effects that shape the way we live our lives. It is for this reason that research informed by ANT is broad ranging and encompasses the relational aspects of power and the ways in which policy circuits operate in practice. The ideas from ANT have been incorporated by scholars in housing economics and cultural geography (e.g., Cook, Smith, and Searle, 2013). The home in this perspective can be seen as an assemblage of artifacts that have relational capabilities with transformative capacity. We return to these themes in Chapter 3.

As part of this overview, we should discuss some of the techniques for data collection. We have already referred to the importance of interviews and observation for research informed by constructionist theories of knowledge, but other methods include discourse analysis and archival research. Discourse analysis pays heed to the performative aspects of language and how powerful groupings are able to deploy to advance their interests. For example, consider the term *housing affordability*. At first glance, this term might appear a neutral one. But its circulation in media and policy settings supports demands from finance industries and developers for more subsidies for home buyers and a relaxation of planning controls. The term *housing affordability* occludes other explanations of the housing crisis, such as the shortfall of public housing and increasing wealth inequality.

Other techniques that have been deployed by housing researchers include historical and archival analysis as a basis to make sense of the contemporary era. One advantage of historical methods is that they make it possible to reflect on the period with the benefit of hindsight. A reflection on the past enables us to differentiate the important from the ephemeral and to notice the continuities and ruptures over a longer trajectory. Without some historical context, it is difficult for researchers to fathom or make sense of what is taking shape in the area of housing.

Finally, though the discipline of economics is influential in discussions of housing markets, the assumptions underpinning economics are that the housing market operates according to principles of supply and demand and that predictions can be made from these. This basic position has come under ever-greater scrutiny in the face of continued housing shortages and the messy role of governments, developers, and banks within this context. Informed economic analyses of housing (Marsh and Gibb, 2011) have focused on the failures of the market to meet the demand for housing and provide more sophisticated models for prediction. Because the price of housing is subject to market forces, explanations usually encompass economics. Of late, interest has resurged in the political economy of housing and the impact of speculative investment in urban property markets in cities such as London, Vancouver, New York, and Sydney.

A political economy approach to housing attends to the broad workings of the economy, in particular the lending practices and investment decisions of banks and finance institutions that determine flows of capital into residential property. The "political economy" approach in recent housing scholarship was set out by academics such as Michael Ball (1983), and of late his work has inspired research on the impact of the global financial crisis for housing outcomes. In short, a political economy approach emphasizes that housing policy initiated by governments prioritizes house prices over and above the needs of low-income households.

Researchers such as Aalbers and Christophers (2014) and Forrest and Hirayama (2014) have also argued that economic uncertainty following the Global Financial Crisis of 2008 has encouraged those with disposable income to invest in housing as an alternative to other products, given its low cost in some areas. The consequence of this investment has been destabilizing for first-time house buyers, who are often unable to compete with investors. Many of those excluded from purchasing property rely on the private rental market for their housing. Other aspects of the housing system shaped by economic factors include the supply of new housing, as the willingness of firms to build new stock depends on such factors as the cost of borrowing and the supply of labor.

Despite the importance of economics, much economic scholarship and research on housing markets has not been acknowledged to any great extent by sociologically informed analysts. In part, this can be attributed to the complexity of economics as a discipline and the fact that most scholars writing on housing draw from the social sciences and geographical traditions. In spite of this, the work of economists such as Thomas Piketty (2014) has generated an interest in tracing the sources of social inequality and the connections to political decision making. In the next chapter, we turn our focus to the meanings of home and the ways that our sense of who we are is shaped by our feelings on home.

Exercises

1. If you could buy any home, what would it look like? What social influences do you think underpin social images of the ideal home?
2. Using our definition of a sociology of housing, what topics would you recommend for urgent investigation by social scientists?
3. What do you think is the ideal home in terms of the society you live in?
4. Now consider your own hopes, identity, and situation—what would be *your* ideal home? Consider its size, layout, and broader situation in a spatial context. Now consider what social and cultural influences are shaping your decisions about what is ideal to you. To what extent do your values mirror those of your parents or those of people around you? What would it mean to choose a very different kind of house or dwelling? How would your friends and family perceive you?
5. What do you think should be the major concerns of housing sociologists?
6. Search for and bring to class an example of a news item that reflects a housing problem or notion of home as an ideal.

Conclusion

In this chapter, we have outlined what we consider are the major concerns of the sociology of housing, and we have also reflected on the way that our homes mediate our experience and contact with wider social structures and forces. We alluded to the critical way in which political and economic systems have come to shape our tenurial preferences and how this is linked to much broader ideas about the sources of wealth, social norms about self-reliance and what it means to own or to rent, and the relative capacity and interest of governments to intervene in some of the key housing problems. Perhaps one of the most wonderfully interesting things about studying such phenomena is that we all, more or less, start from some degree of expertise in these issues. We all have a story to tell about our personal experiences, and these experiences can help us to begin to understand a much broader range of issues and problems.

A sociology of housing concerns itself with homelessness, the loss of home, the politics of housing, and even our needs within the wider social world and its physical dwelling environments. Writing at a time of massive social and economic upheaval, we can see how relevant housing is to concerns about human welfare, and we witness the relative frailty of entire societies built upon economies in which the ownership of housing was normatively constructed as something essential, and that to fail to own was itself a kind of social failure. These issues should give us some inkling of the deep importance of housing and its role in determining economic outcomes that shape and constrain our personal life histories.

Seen in these different ways, the home is the hub of a whole complex of relationships and in many ways the crucial medium through which society is structured and constructed for us. We are socialized by one or more parents at home, and we view media systems in the home's comfortable surroundings, armed with knowledge and insights from these sources in ways that make us more or less accomplished social actors who go on to engage with other personal and institutional settings that further our sense of self—but we always return home! It is where we start and end our day, and its quality, location, size, prestige, and structure shape in large part our satisfaction or concern with our own lives. These points should help us to see how utterly vital sociological interest with houses, homes, and societies is and the kind of contribution that a theoretically informed and empirically robust set of studies may have to contribute for society, policy makers, and governments that need to see the nature and routes out of various housing problems. As Saunders and Williams argued in their agenda-setting piece some decades ago:

> Houses are the crucible of the social system, the base point around which local and national politics is organised and which in essence provides the starting basis for the allocation and distribution of resources, the collection of statistics and much else besides. It is all of these things, certainly, but first and foremost it is the nodal point of our society, the locale through which individual and society interact. (1988: 84)

The following chapter considers the work of social researchers and brings together relevant treatments of the home to assemble a coherent and distinctive concept of houses and homes in their wider social contexts.

3 The Meaning of Home

Introduction

The home is often considered to be a place of private expression and personal autonomy, a major and intrinsic part of modern human identity. Of course, our homes satisfy fundamental needs and desires that are common to most of us, operating as sites of decoration and display, as developmental markers of rebellion in the case of teenagers (primarily through the bedroom) but also to feelings of sanctuary and group identity (see also the discussion in Chapter 4). The way homes are designed for us and subsequently inscribed by us as their residents reflect deeply embedded cultural norms and the ways in which social class is subtly encoded in these spaces (Highmore, 2014). The home is also situated in sociolegal frameworks and definitions (Fox, 2002) that shape the meaning of the home and shared understandings of the rights we have to enjoy such spaces, to enjoy protection from intrusion or the possibility of it being seized (an issue that is crucial to anxieties and developments in countries like China and much of sub-Saharan Africa). Rules of housing law remain important, even where we "own" the title and dwelling erected on its material substrate. When we rent our home from a landlord, housing law provides us with protection from the specter of eviction and privacy to occupy the home in a way of our choosing. These understandings of the meaning of home as a place of sanctuary, privacy, and other key rights are critical to the ways in which we understand notions of ownership, renting, and the rights to home more generally (we revisit many of these issues in Chapter 5 while examining the loss of the home).

Society and social norms flow into the microcosm of society in which the home is just one component. The claim we make by ourselves to and upon our own homes (whether we own them or rent them) often reflects the tastes, habits, and dispositions of our parents, friends, and social circles more broadly. Our rights to home do not extinguish the equivalent rights of other parties who enter our homes or inhabit them without clear legal recourse, as demonstrated in some court cases where intruders have managed to sue property owners for breaches in the latter's duty of care. This can be a significant issue in situations where parties are forced to share a home even when tensions are fierce—for teenagers and parents or couples working their way through a property settlement after an agreement to separate. For example, such issues are now recognized in understandings of the right to a home and the subsequent obligation of governments to provide housing. In international law, the meaning of home is understood as a space of shelter from harm and is enshrined in the 1948 United Nations Universal Declaration of Human Rights. Article 12 of the declaration stipulates, "No one shall be subjected to arbitrary interference with his privacy, family, home, or correspondence ...," and Article 25 states, "Everyone has the right to a standard of living adequate for the health and well-being of himself and of his family, including food, clothing, housing and medical care and necessary social services ..."

In this chapter, we explore the home as the fundamental place that offers a sense of both refuge and possibilities, safe from the strictures of public life and social conformity, while it also retains the sense of being a space through which broader social currents run deeply and affect us in ways that we might deny publicly. What our home means to us and signifies to others more broadly is often deeply bound to notions of ownership and design. Within Anglophone cultures, the ideologically preferred idea and image of home remains the "single-family dwelling," as we discussed earlier, often depicted as the solid, secure backdrop to a photo-portrait of father, mother, children, new car, and perhaps a pet or two. Regardless of how we live and grow up, this image retains a powerful influence, a well-functioning hegemonic frame that shapes how we think about what we should aim for in life and how buildings exert considerable influence over us, offering the lure of a personal dream about the ideal personal or family life that is shared by many others competing for the work rewards to secure these goals.

These embedded ideas about home thus structure our experience of life more generally, indicating to us to what extent we match up to an ideal and see ourselves as being more or less successful. For those more or less caught up in these social goals, the physical space and exterior of the home is taken as a mark—of success, failure, or deviation from those norms. The catch is that we live in deeply unequal and divided societies in which the resources necessary to access such homes are limited, as is the availability of such homes in the first place. As many analysts now recognize, declining levels of home ownership not only place a new burden on governments wishing to appear as though they can facilitate the dreams of all to own, new waves of renting among young people are now embraced as a form of positive deviation from widely held norms, fatalistically retreating into new sociotenurial identities in which goals of ownership are rejected, in part because they enable a sense of personal social value in a new landscape of precarious labor and runaway housing costs (Standing, 2011). Despite these changes, the relative supply of what economists call "positional goods" (the fixed availability of relatively few goods that act as displays of social status such as large or detached homes in central London means that only relatively few can win the race to achieve these.

Our ability to attain decent homes, let alone those that confer status and good social standing, may also be under threat. In the new megacities across the globe, dense inner-city agglomerations of apartments and condominiums highlight that not only are very different kinds of dwelling being normalized (informal shanty developments and high rise [Graham, 2004]), but also that competition for such resources has become acute or even unbearable for many. In cities like London and Hong Kong (and to a slightly lesser extent in Sydney and Melbourne), the cost of housing has multiplied to between 15 and 20 times the average household earnings. The meaning and possibility of home under such conditions is highly constrained and highlighted by the re-emergence of early twentieth-century patterns of continued residence in the parental home.

Sociologists have been keen to argue that despite what some (e.g., Saunders, 1990) deem an innate desire and the self-evident advantages of home ownership (via rights of control, continuity of tenure, and the possibilities of personal wealth gains), these positions rarely stand up to cross-cultural or legal scrutiny. The rights of tenants in many European countries are much more secure and detailed, whereas the wealth of owners in Anglosphere countries has historically been inflated and maintained by preferential government treatments through macroeconomic policies such as tax subsidies for landlords, first-time home buyer grants, sandbagging of housing wealth from public pension eligibility tests, stamp duty suspension, and so forth. In sum, this chapter is a discussion of the wider significance of these diverse meanings and an exploration of how ideologies serve to maintain particular constructions and narratives of the home.

The "politics" of home

How should we define the variegated meanings of home? A helpful way to consider the meanings of home is put forward by Blunt and Dowling (2006: 2–3). They argue that "home is: a place/site, a set of feelings/cultural meanings, as well as consisting of the relations between the two." Their conceptualization is helpful for showing why the home means more than a physical dwelling; it features as part of our deeper social imaginary. Hence it is common for us to feel sentimental or nostalgic when we think of home and associate it with comfort and privacy. Of course this is not always the case. As we stated in our introduction, the home can also be a site of discomfort and unhappiness, a place where bad things and violence may happen, or in a more mundane way, a socially stifling place that binds us to unwanted, outmoded traditions of parents or extended kin networks. At times our home may appear to have lost its usefulness, its value diminished due to economic factors like local de-industrialization, political determinants such as war or occupation, or even a simple zoning change.

In recent years, researchers have made much of the importance of the material home within the wider political domain, seeking, for example, to gauge its significance for accentuating or arresting inequality (Dorling, 2014). The political component of home was of great interest to Pierre Bourdieu (1984 and 1993); he argued that the wider significance of home is externally imposed by a combination of consumer values and political ideology. Bourdieu developed the concept of "habitus" to understand the sense of self and identity we derive from living in the home. In *Distinction* (1984) and *The Field of Cultural Production* (1993), he argued that *where* and *how* people choose to reside is significant because it enables us to display difference in relation to values that are established in the productive economy. Bourdieu's concept of habitus directs our attention to the centrality of relationships and values in decisions about the home. The choices and values we hold cannot be reduced to economic rationality as they entail self-reflection and an assessment of our circumstances.

Doreen Massey (1995) also provides a valuable perspective, suggesting that the home can be viewed through the prism of power geometries. Massey's claim is that our domiciles are politicized sites of conflict in which claims are made on space, modes of use, and configuration. The length of time occupying the bathroom, the volume of music played through speakers, and personal belongings deposited in the living room are examples of conflicts that are played out by teenagers who co-habit with their parent(s), for instance. As we will discuss in Chapter 4, teenage children often feel the pressure and presence of their parents' authority as stifling and oppressive and seek privacy in the controlled spaces of their bedrooms or other demarcated zones within the home. This withdrawal into nonparentally monopolized space can be enough to restore a sense of justice and self-esteem to the fragile teenage self.

This micropolitics of intra-home occupation and control is also evident in the increasing popularity of the men's shed movement. Men's sheds provide a venue to restore bicycles, make furniture, salvage cars, and idle away time. Most of the people who use these locations tend to be retired tradesman, blue-collar or process workers looking for a non-market space in which to continue the practices of their productive lives on their own terms at last, maintaining the preponderant self-image that they take from their careers in the service of making things.

Power relationships in the home often conform to culturally informed gender roles; for example, traditionally, the leadership (head) of the household is assigned to the man of the house—"an Englishman's home is his castle"—while women take on the role of principal carers for family and children. Of course, this has implications for ownership, control, or responsibility for particular spaces in the home. Traditionally, much of this has related to the drudgery and ownership of space by women in unpaid working relations (Oakley, 1974a), but recently much has been made of the complex temporal and gendered use of particular spaces and changing roles between the sexes. For example, sociologists have begun to highlight how the "front region" of the living room, often identified as a space for public display of the self, is increasingly managed in ways that householders view as serving their needs more directly, thus suggesting at least partially that the internal spaces of the home are being remade in line with complex renegotiations of the ways in which social contact is managed from and within the home (Miller, 2008).

At the individual level, new forms of isolation can be identified within domestic spaces. Zygmunt Bauman (2000) writes of the increased sense of anomie among young people as employment opportunities diminish and give way to a competitive culture that strains traditional bonds of sociality. Sociologists such as Adrian Franklin (2012) have noted that commercial businesses such as Facebook capitalize on feelings of anomie and isolation (Franklin, 2012) by holding out the allure of virtual friendships through their social media platforms. The surge in people communicating on instant messaging sites such as Twitter signifies new cultural practices that are changing archaic face-to-face or more recent voice-to-voice forms of human interaction. It is common now to refer to one's Facebook site as a "home page" on the Web, and the proprietors of the system spend considerable sums of money on constant upgrades and alterations to the technology so that it continues to appear "shiny," cutting edge, attractive, and easy to navigate. On reflection, the "concrete" practices associated with homemaking (defragging instead of spring cleaning, changing monitor backgrounds instead of gardening, design makeovers, and fire walls instead of feature walls or indeed "real" fire walls) are now a feature of these new technologies. The structure of homemaking is thus being extended and reproduced in the growing virtual universe of capitalist enterprise with personal identity shaped and manicured in domestic settings via our online presence.

At least since the late 1970s, scholars like Christopher Lasch, Anthony Giddens, Zygmunt Bauman, Slavoj Zizek, David Harvey, Ulrich Beck, Richard Sennett, Jane Jacobs, and Robert Putnam have written widely on an alleged growing retreat in the West from the realm of collectivity, commons, or public sphere into a private, monadic, solipsistic, or narcissistic preoccupation with self-esteem and individual advancement within established structures such as government or corporations, identity politics, "reality" television, and in the reflected glows of celebrity and consumerism. These changes can be identified as a kind of widespread form of social privatism in which the home, because of social, economic, and technological changes, has taken on an increasing primacy in the lives of many people who are shunning social contact and face-to-face connections in the community (Putnam, 2007) and seeking entertainment and personal release in films, hobbies, domestic drinking, dinner parties, and pornography, facilitated by the increasing use of domestic delivery systems for almost any and all products and services. The point is neither to condemn nor celebrate these changes, but to note how the great indoors (Highmore, 2014) of the home is increasingly a space that promises at least in principle to satisfy and activate a wide range of desires and needs that can be sated through the home's increasing connection with a more knowing and responsive capitalism.

The net result of many of these changes has been to move many previously social and public functions into the interior spaces of the home. In recent years, we have witnessed a disengagement from representative forms of politics and the adoption of a more cynical attitude. The retreat from collectivity is mirrored by the turn toward the private sphere and the home. Again, we can attribute these changes to the influence exerted by the ideology of neoliberalism and what Nikolas Rose has termed the "disciplining of the subject" (Rose, 2000). Rose deploys this term to describe how governments have encouraged us to

reject modes of collective belonging in favor of an ill-defined individualism. Hence the shift toward the home as a site of security and retreat
becomes even more significant. The home both as a retreat from politics and a place of consumption is encouraged. Under these conditions,
social norms of privatism, the private home as a form of potential economic gain through its resale, and an increasing awareness by citizen-
consumers of the methods of buying and selling homes for such gain
suggests we might view the space of the home as a kind of tessellated
building block of these sociopolitical systems (the notion of a property-
owning democracy so often trumpeted in the frontier capitalist societies). The connection of home and citizen suggests a complex interplay
of political values and beliefs in which ownership implies a kind of
relative social withdrawal from the public domain outside (Atkinson
and Blandy, 2016).

Situating the home in the setting of a wider political economy brings
to our notice the inherent problems with postulating binary categories
or oppositions. It is not uncommon in sociological research to view
the home through the prism of binaries, for example, public or private,
home or unhomely, housed or homeless, home or away, and mobile
or sedentary. Binaries have appeal because of their simplicity, but they
are inadequate for capturing the complexities of the home. Instead, we
suggest the meaning of home encompasses *performativity, experiences*,
and *representation*s. This continuum of performativity, experience, and
representation enables us to fathom the geographic, physical, practical, and ideational components of home in ways that are navigable.
The frame of performativity encourages us to identify the activities of
"homemaking" and other associated practices enacted in spaces associated with home. *Experience* enables us to consider feelings about home
that surface at times of upheaval, for example, during migration or
moving, as well as the feelings of attachment that many of us have concerning home. Much notable literature exists on the home; for example, the work of Daniel Miller (2008, 2010) seeks to consider how the
home and objects within the home engender feelings of belonging and
attachment.

Understanding home as a set of experiences and feelings encompasses
the work of scholars such as Bauman (2000), Urry (2000), and Cresswell
(2006). Each sees the home as a site of stability in opposition to the
world of the social that is increasingly mobile and in flux. The subject's
disconnection from the stability of home and place is a defining feature
of the modern age for Bauman. He traces much of the anxiety and ennui
to changes in the form of capitalist development that have led to more

flexible forms of labor and new technologies that have replaced face-to-face encounters as forms of sociability have changed, and new anxieties about social being and economic continuity or growth have been generated in the public domain and from which the private home is often viewed as being counterposed or emancipated (see Hiscock, Kearns, Macintyre, and Ellaway, 2010).

Traditionally, some scholars interested in housing have been content to limit their research to a defined set of parameters. Housing policy and the production of housing have been the main foci, with only a marginal interest in housing consumption. Housing was viewed either through the prism of tenure and the sociolegal rights of its inhabitants or as just a physical artifice. One consequence was the considerable body of scholarship that sought to consider how our housing tenure shapes social and class identities (see Rex and Moore, 1967), the idea of what was known as housing classes, and sociolegal research that considered the way that tenure has impacts on rights, and the assumptions around such concepts as "citizenship" and "property" (see Blandy and Goodchild, 1999).

Much has changed over the last thirty years or so, and contemporary sociological scholarship is both theoretically informed and wide-ranging in its scope. In recent years, sociologists have spent considerable time debating the meaning of home (Mallett, 2006) and assessing its significance in terms of individual identity and society at large. There has been much confusion, with some researchers seeking to impose tight definitions while others use terms like *home* and *house* interchangeably, with little regard for precision. For purposes of analytical clarity, it is helpful to distinguish the concept of home as a lens to make sense of people's *performances/practices* and *experience/understandings* from the *material* dwelling of home (for more on this, see Chapter 1). As previously suggested, another distinction we can make concerns the *representation* of the home in popular culture and the individual experience of home. Although experience and representation of home are mutually bounded, the distinction is helpful as representations of home are in the public/societal realm, whereas experiences are by definition always individuated. Finally, we can categorize place as the site or setting in which the home is situated. Confusion can be avoided if we bear in mind these distinctions (see Table 3.1). In the remainder of this chapter, we cover the range of subjective meanings of home, provide examples of the how home is used in everyday settings, and outline ways home design shapes both societal relationships and our interactions with technologies.

Table 3.1 Typologies of home

Ideational	Experiences	Interiority, subjective experience of home
	Representations	Cultural, media and artistic representations of the home
Material	Material Dwelling	Shelter, home
	Place	Neighborhood/ Community Site of home
	Performativity/practices	Homemaking practices, DIY, Cooking

Although our perspectives of home are formed subjectively, our understandings are always shaped by wider cultural processes and our own life trajectories. It is for that reason, the way we view home and how we use it is always in flux. Think of how children view the home and how our views change radically as we age. It is important to understand that the home generates affects or emotions. For example, some of us feel attachment to a home, though at times in our lives we might be desperate to escape from it. In the remainder of this chapter, we consider common feelings that arise with respect to home.

Owning and renting

Our feelings of home are always affected by our circumstances. One of the major debates in recent sociological scholarship relates to the claims made by some writers, such as Saunders (1990) who has argued that owning a home generates a greater sense of attachment, and this is why so many of us have a desire to own rather than rent. Saunders's work has been criticized by many commentators (e.g., Somerville, 1989; Hiscock et al., 2010) for not incorporating ways that governments have promoted home ownership through tax incentives and other discounts. In addition, the finance industry, seeking ways to boost profits, has had great success in advertising the benefits of home ownership in ways that appeal to our sense of insecurity. Recall the TV advertisements enticing young people to acquire mortgages. In short, there is an ideology of home ownership that shapes our feelings of the home.

Economic conditions or change in individual circumstances can dramatically affect our view of home. For example, if we lose our job and struggle to meet the mortgage payments, our view of home can radically alter. Rather than being our prized asset, the cost of servicing a mortgage debt can change the way we feel toward our home. Our feelings of the home can also be transformed following a dramatic event, such as a split relationship or children leaving the family home. Even a long journey or for migrants a trip to their former home may alter feelings of home.

Cultural issues and wider politics are not confined to issues of home ownership. As we discuss in forthcoming chapters, renting in public housing or in the private sector is culturally specific. In countries such as the United Kingdom, the United States, New Zealand, and Australia, renting is often framed negatively, particularly with regard to social housing (Dupuis and Thorns, 2002). However, in other countries such as Switzerland and Germany, the social stigma of renting is much less prevalent and, unlike in the United Kingdom, large institutional corporations are willing to invest in housing for rent. For these reasons, feelings about renting and owning are culturally specific and not innate, but they are also shaped by the economic contexts, and potential financial benefits of ownership generated by macroeconomic policies, such as interest-rate settings, that have often been used by governments ensure that ownership is affordable and can be encouraged.

Housing has traditionally been produced as a commodity that is sold to an owner-occupier or landlord, and yet over the last thirty years, it has increasingly become an investment vehicle to accrue wealth as well as a place to live, and this has changed what home means for its inhabitants. Those who own their homes usually anticipate that they will appreciate not just the pleasures of living in the home but also a growing potential return on the investment that may accrue over time as the value of their home increases. In recent years, we have witnessed an increased commodification of the home. No longer viewed entirely as a site of privacy, the home has become viewed as a space for transaction and consumption. We can see this in the way that TV programs focus on the home as sites for buying and selling of property and cooking, although DIY and gardening are the most common uses (Allon, 2011). The home is now a place where many households have an office, and some employees favor working from home as a way to reduce costs.

The increasingly commercialized nature of domestic life has been shaped, in part, by the influence of an ideology of home ownership. Like other nation-states, contemporary Britain has become socially atomized, but these changes are also evident at a number of levels. For example, at the neighborhood level, it is not unusual for households to seek ways to bolster their privacy through fences, gates, and security configurations. And though it would be wrong to assume that the desire for privacy is always congruent with a desire for social isolation, the fixation on security suggests a heightened level of mistrust toward neighbors. We can also note that many households with high incomes seek to live in homogeneous suburbs and choose schools for their children that confirm their class position. The impact of these choices is profound, not least because they entrench and also extend long-standing social fissures.

As Nicole Cook and her colleagues have shown (see Cook, Smith, and Searle, 2013), these financial and material aspects of the home are intertwined. They draw on the earlier work of Jacobs and Smith (2008), deploying the term *housing assemblage* to illuminate the home as "a site of emergence, something which is produced, performed and in a state of always becoming through a seamless web of activity and engagement in a more-than-human world" (Cook et al., 2013: 3). Financial products are now available for owners to draw equity from their home to spend on other goods and services. As Cook et al. (2013: 3) write, "Financial flows form the skeleton on which the assemblage of home hangs. Financial products and services, along with practices of borrowing and repayment, play a key role in maintaining this assemblage." A vast array of such activities stems from the housing assemblage emanating from financial transactions, for example, including holidays, cars, furnishings, and renovations.

Symbolic and relational meaning

Much of the recent literature on the home has considered the *symbolic* aspects of home. By this we mean the way that home serves to represent aspects of our identity and being in the world. So, for example, middle-class households who live in Victorian houses in areas associated with gentrification derive pleasure from the status that their home confers. In other words, homes are not merely practical as a place of shelter but also have symbolic function in terms of the way we want to display our identities and convey meaning.

Objects and the home

Objects in the home also have symbolic significance; for example, works of art are displayed because they give us some pleasure from viewing their form, but also because they can remind us of associations or connections or convey what Bourdieu terms "cultural capital." Photographs and old mementos displayed on the mantelpieces of migrant living rooms are examples of objects that maintain significance. The focus on symbolic meanings of home and its objects has provided a rich vein of scholarship, but there is a strand of research that seeks to consider how the home generates "relational" affects as well as symbolic ones. Much of the work here draws upon the anthropologist Daniel Miller (2008), who argues that the attributes of objects generate meaning through our relational encounters with them. Miller's work has implications for housing scholarship (for a discussion, see Jacobs and Malpass, 2011) in that it foregrounds attention on the way that identity and meaning are only formed *in relation* to something else. Therefore, the home and its objects are sometimes viewed as if they are human, as when we give our houses names and think of homes having biographies as spaces in which key elements of personal and family life are periodized. Thomas (1991: 125) has argued that "as socially and culturally salient entities, objects change in defiance of their material stability. The category to which a thing belongs, the emotion and judgment it prompts, and narrative it recalls, are all historically refigured." For Thomas, the significance of objects has less to do with what they were designed for and more with what they become.

Home as a physical artifact

As stated at the start of the chapter, sociologists have viewed the home materially, as a base from which individuals can seek shelter. One consequence of this conceptualization is the work undertaken on homelessness generally construed as the absence of a physical roof over one's head. The discussion of housing in terms of its physicality generally explores architectural or design features (see Nuttgens, 1989). Recognition that the material aspect of home is only one component of what constitutes it has encouraged scholars to extend the scope of inquiry to the home as imaginary—particularly those interested in the meaning of home in the context of postcolonial experiences and migration (see Blunt and Dowling, 2006).

Exercises

One of our objectives in this chapter has been to encourage you to see the home in a wider context. The following questions are deliberately broad so as to encourage you to think of the ways the home constitutes an imaginary construct through which we are able to establish identity.

1. Consider the objects in your home: Do they have any impact about the meaning you attach to your experience of home?
2. Does it matter what home means to different individuals and social groups?
3. Why do so many people attach significance to *where* we live?
4. What does the obsession with home tell us about the way we live and the modern era?

Conclusion

In this chapter, we have advanced an understanding of home as more than simple bricks and mortar. We have suggested that the home occupies a space in which we imbue our feelings and aspirations in relation to self-identity and also in relation to others and the environment. As stated earlier, discussions on home can be confusing if we conflate home as a sociological concept to understand society with the symbolic and relational meanings of home as a physical dwelling. Sociologists have often sought to provide typologies of the home to make sense of the wide range of meanings. Yet there is much to be said for the arguments of Rapoport (2001) that the concept of home has only limited heuristic value because of its vagueness and inherent subjectivity (for a discussion, see Fox O'Mahony, 2007, 2012).

This noted, a sociological investigation of the meaning of home provides an entrée to some of the wider debates of the current era, encompassing issues such as globalization, the nation state, inequality, and personal identity. Perhaps the best way to see home is in relation to, rather than as, a site in which we imbue meaning. In other words, the meaning of home only becomes actualized in relation to material objects, including persons. Home therefore not only comprises a sense of place but also a broad set of feelings (Blunt and Dowling, 2006: 254).

In some respects, we can see one of the tasks of sociology is to consider the broad meanings of home and their wider significance. Blunt and Dowling make the important point that we must resist positing binaries, dualisms, or oppositions such as private or public, home or homelessness, homely or unhomely, urban or suburban, state or market, and so on. Rather, we should see meanings of home along a continuum that combines experiences and representation. Finally, when reflecting on the meaning of home, we need to be vigilant regarding the manner in which home is experienced and distinguish this from its representation across the media of arts, politics, and culture. As we have suggested, the meaning of home and the subjective experience of home are closely related, and the meaning of home is always shaped by popular representations of home; in turn, these popular versions are shaped by the individual meanings we hold.

4 The Household, Gender and Sexuality

One of the fascinating aspects of how we live is the way we imbue our lives as a journey; moving forward in time as we age, we collect memories and acquire knowledge. This construction of the self is a feature of Western modernity, and the home plays an important component to this identity construction. For many, the home in this narrative serves as an imagined sanctuary, a place we can escape the ravages of capitalism. Yet this imaginary is not approximate to many whose homes are a site of labor, conflict, and much more. As Michael and Garver (2009: 361) write, the home "is a space of sequestration and connection, a place of pleasure and rationalization, a site of ordinariness and uniqueness— each of these is patterned in historically and culturally specific ways."

Socially, we can see the home as a formation making and changing the way we engage with each other and ourselves. It is a truism to observe that households change through the life course of each person, but as we are living longer, so there are more single households, higher rates of divorce, and more complex relationships than those found in the traditional family. It is not uncommon for parents at some stage to choose to live apart, engage in more porous relationships, and adopt different methods of child-rearing. All these new practices are indicative of the difficulties many of us have conforming to the idealization of a nuclear family while yearning to break out and experiment.

It is helpful to view household change in historical context. During the first demographic transition in the late nineteenth century, household sizes decreased because of a decline in fertility rates, though mortality rates also fell at this time. Since the 1960s, there have been significant changes leading some demographers to use the term *second demographic transition* as they witnessed higher rates of divorce, extra-marital births, and cohabitation. There are also more elderly people living alone and more same-sex couples and couples living apart, together (LAT) in separate dwellings (Simpson, 2012). In the world of work, there has been a large increase in women working in the labor market, and it is common for couples to pursue dual careers. Although we would not wish to advance a technological deterministic explanation, it is clear that to some extent the demographic changes can be sourced to changes in technology (labor-saving devices), new production techniques (post-Fordist economy), and biomedical advances (contraception pill) that have enabled women to secure jobs, acquire income, and become less dependent on men. These technological changes in the modes of production facilitated service industry sectors in the United Kingdom, which led to new consumption and leisure activities; young people had greater purchasing power and were more able to participate in higher education, and so on. There has also been an increase in labor mobility as a result of economic conditions and the housing market. These developments in the UK economy are also a component of wider global changes in capitalist development that have led to multinational industries moving production sites to nation-states with cheaper labor costs. The UK manufacturing industries have declined since the 1980s and been superseded by financial and other related service industries.

Households are very different from a hundred years ago. The most significant demographic change is that more people live longer and on their own. In the last twenty years, there has been a large increase in children remaining at home into their adult years. In part, this reflects difficulties in accessing affordable accommodations and securing well-paid employment.

Thus far, we covered general ideas about home and household, but it is impossible to consider the role of the domestic home without assessing its impacts on the different subgroups within it, specifically, how men and women share and divide the responsibilities of its management and upkeep. We can think about these issues from a number of perspectives. For Marxist scholars, the home is a unit of labor reproduction, the site through which current and future workers are nourished, prepared, and rested—that is, readied for work—and critically, a site in which the work of women is unpaid and unrecognized as the foundation of the wider capitalist economy (Dalla Costa and James, 1973; Eisenstein, 1999). In this context, women's contribution to the household was also critical for wider capital accumulation and imperial expansion, yet unrecognized by pay or in social value. Since the 1960s, the home has also been the site of perspectives foregrounding the female experience of life in the home, often under broader social conditions of patriarchy, and thereby the home is a repressive and constricting experience, emphasized by the drudgery and repetition of household tasks (Oakley, 1974b), the lack of autonomy, and routines of preparing others in the household and the politics surrounding cooking, child-rearing, and sex.

Bringing these issues up to date requires further insight into the increasingly diverse range of household types and family arrangements that have developed due to new social processes including partner separation, divorce, so-called household dissolution (the need for multiple homes following family breakups), and among other examples, trends like "living together, apart." A consideration of sexualities also requires us to question how we should continue to aspire to or think of "typical" modes of social existence within the home and also how identities shape patterns of usage, the meaning of home and household formation today (Duyvendak, 2011). Similarly, the rise of personal anxieties and workplace insecurities has generated new forms of anomie. It is apparent that for many young people drugs and alcohol serve as a form of self-medication in an anxiety-inducing social world in which few assurances remain (Winlow and Hall, 2013).

How we understand the home has changed significantly over the last forty years. The living arrangements and the social relationships formed within the home were largely framed as "private" and of little concern to sociologists until the 1960s. The lack of interest in the home can be contrasted with the interest in the world of work. Sociologists such as Blauner (1964) and Braverman (1974) reached a wider audience through their research on industry and labor relations. These early ideas remain influential, particularly the way in which many people wish to regard the home as a personal space and uphold a distinction between "public" and "private," bounded by the edges of the physical dwelling itself. In this light, we have internalized the idea that the home is a site of sanctuary and domesticity, a place where we can exclude others and protect ourselves (Atkinson and Blandy, 2016). However, one of the major contributions of feminist scholarship has been to pry open this distinction between the world of work and home and establish a more fluid and layered understanding of what constitutes the home, particularly the idea that the home may be identified as an escape from an outer world of work. In this chapter, we cast aside readings of domesticity as somehow separate from work and discuss the relationships that are constituted in the setting of home. These include gender and sexual roles, lifestyles, and everyday social practices, more broadly. The location of home *contra* work is redundant; primarily for women, home has always been a place of work, with increasingly porous boundaries made even more possible by new communication technologies. Around a quarter of British employees now work from home one day a week, but this apparent revolution in work practice has not caught on in the way that many analysts had initially predicted (Gorz, 1982) as the vast majority of full-time workers still travel to their place of employment.

Economists now recognize that home is central to the operation of the economy and has a primary role in facilitating capitalist production. The relationships within the home not only effect wider societal change but are also shaped by societal change. In specific terms, as Simpson (2012: 227) suggests, "Consumption practices and mobility patterns of households shape urban development and the built environment." For example, the need for relative proximity of the workplace and child care, particular for dual-earning households, has shaped demands for transportation systems and a search in the private housing market for locations that optimize the social and economic needs of households (Bartley, Blanton, and Gilliard, 2005). These patterns are increasingly complex, and rising house prices have further exaggerated the need of many families to place both partners in work, both as a form of social emancipation as well as a response to service the required mortgage debt that might help realize their dreams for the right kind of home (Jarvis, 1999).

The family and the household

As noted, until the 1970s, only scant attention was afforded to the spaces within the home (Tufte and Myerhoff, 1979). Housing was largely viewed in relation to the wider community and its role in capitalist production, a reflection perhaps of the patriarchal assumptions that underpinned sociological research at the time. The home as a topic of serious investigation can be traced to the work of feminist scholars such as Friedan, Oakley, Hayden, and Greer. Their work on issues such as domestic labor, patriarchy, and the lack of recognition of women's work inspired a later generation of feminist scholars to consider the home as a site of social and gendered conflict, as well as one of violence and interpersonal repression. Particular importance was attached to the "lived" experience of the home and its role in identity formation. Feminist scholarship paved the way for future investigations into sexuality, the meaning of home and identity, and the way that home is represented discursively.

The contribution of feminist scholarship has been immense; over the last thirty years, there have been wide ranging investigations on varied issues such as domestic violence, gender, sexual identity, and

homemaking. The notion of home in the making of sexual and gendered identity has been a critical focus, how hegemonic constructions of
breadwinners and homemakers reinforce traditional binaries and how
the home creates possibilities for alternative identities forged in opposition to heteronormativity (Bell and Valentine, 1995). As we have stated,
the long-held distinctions between home and work, home and homeless, public and private, male and female, are much more fluid than
previously imagined. Feminist scholarship has shown that the formal
distinctions we make between public and private spaces, though not
redundant, are not as significant as previously thought. The home is
now increasingly a place of work and an integral component of capitalist production (Armstrong and Squires, 2002).

Gender and lifestyles

The home is not simply a container in which lifestyles are enacted;
rather, it is coterminous in their making. For example, watching television has been an enduring feature of home life for decades, and in
recent years, computers and mobile technologies have also proliferated.
Technological devices encourage and even solicit us to engage in ways
that facilitate consumption from the home; TV is placed center stage in
the living room to facilitate sociality and sharing. Michael and Garver
(2009: 361) have explored devices such as the TV and computer "epoch-
ally reshaping people's relations to the world 'beyond' the home." They
argue that these technologies have turned people into "saturated selves"
in multishifting and linking different modes of being. Often this can
lead to a changing sense of self-identity that is less predicated on real-
time human relationships and more reliant on narratives enacted across
media platforms.

Because it is clear that the technologies of the home facilitate lifestyles, what are the dominant ones of the contemporary era? We can
note a number of home stereotypes. The archetypal "swinging bach-
elor," a single man living in a small flat who seeks intimacy through
sociality has been supplemented with new and gendered versions. For
example, there is the domestic goddess, given articulation through TV
programs on cooking, hosted by Nigella Lawson or by Rachael Ray in
the United States. Other lifestyles include the stay-at-home mother, the
homeworker, and the teenage nerd on his computer all day. For children
or teenagers, the home during the evening is often a place of no alternative, as they are deemed too young to frequent bars and clubs. Young

teenagers often congregate in bedrooms, listening to music on shared devices (Fisher, 2009; Furlong, 2008). In many ways, these processes have been reinforced by parental anxieties about the personal safety and moral corruptibility of middle-class children (Currie, 2005; Letiecq and Koblinsky, 2004) and also by the fears of young people in high crime areas (Rossen et al., 2011).

Two other powerful home stereotypes are the "handyman," in which men take responsibility for "home maintenance," and the "stay-at-home" housewife. The fact that the "handyman" has endured is testimony to the fact that gendered divisions still operate and may also be attributable to male anxiety over failure to perform well in most other arenas of domestic work. The garden shed (the preserve of those fortunate enough to have a garden) becomes a DIY (do-it-yourself) site as well as a refuge from the activities of the home.

For much of the first part of the twentieth century the "stay-at-home" mother was normalized in middle-class cultural settings. Yet this construction has waned among the middle classes as more women enter the labor market. There are other iconic images of what we can call home identities, such as the teenage rebel who establishes an identity in opposition to his or her parents through identification with pop music, motorbikes, fashion, and so on. These identities were often forged in the spaces of the home, but they ultimately require public display to achieve shared validation. The home identities that we are so familiar with do require a public to be actualized.

Pink (2004) provides a useful discussion using charted home practices. Home practices are inseparable from the productive formations inherent in capitalism. The lifestyles associated with the home are like the home itself—porous in that they are infused with the ideas, practices, and discourses in general circulation. But lifestyles can be viewed as idealizations that we seek to conform to or reject. Hence, we aspire to be the good father or mother, homemakers, engaging in practices that we think are required to achieve this ideal. The logic of capitalism requires us to strive constantly but ultimately falls short; therefore, we must acquire new goods to attain a closer resemblance to these lifestyles. Although it would be wrong to equate hard work with drudgery, what is often concealed in these popular stereotypical lifestyles is the labor entailed behind the front door of the home: the serene couple striving to produce the perfect dinner-party ambience; the teenagers searching for new products and experiences from tablets in their bedrooms; or the status-seeking professionals, painstakingly seeking to assemble the urban residence that might somehow match their readings of the homes in magazines or on television. This produces ambivalence about these socially derived and influential images of lifestyle as a way of being and the attempt to carve out more authentic existences that might be free of persistent media messages and social norms. But even authenticity as a concept has been subject to commodification, and Marxist theory has been influential here in offering an awareness of the way in which capitalism successfully creates desires and our sense of "lack" as one of the primary motivations for consumption (Adorno and Horkheimer, 1997).

Home spaces

The way that gendered constructions retain influence is apparent when we consider the spaces within the home. The kitchen has endured largely as a female or family space in which cooking takes place. In recent years, the kitchen has become more important as a place to socialize; it is the place where residents are happy to receive guests. An obvious reason for the prominence of the kitchen is the value we now attach to cooking and informality. The formal spaces of the home are no longer seen as in vogue.

It is not only the kitchen that has attained importance. Other rooms become symbolically and relationally significant. The living room is a place to display the household wares and per Bourdieu (1984 and 1993), the meanings we imbue in objects reflect wider values and practices of consumption. Bourdieu's interest in objects of the home lay primarily in their significance for displaying difference. Bourdieu's work remains influential, but fascinating research exists in a collection of essays edited by Daniel Miller (2001). The collection displays how everyday objects not only generate meaning but actually form relational encounters that engender notions of identity. The object displayed on a mantelpiece therefore represents something of symbolic importance but also establishes a relationship with the owner that furnishes selfhood.

Identities and sexuality in relation to the home

The norms associated with heterosexuality feature in many of the discourses surrounding the home. Common media representations feature the home as a site of family togetherness, often in suburban locations. As Gorman-Murray (2008) noted, the house is idealized as a setting in which heterosexual relationships are maintained and the family reproduced. This version of the home is idealized but also actively reproduced in the architecture of home design (kitchens, master and children's bedrooms) and the design of suburbs (detached, with gardens for play). Until recently, housing finance was predicated on the traditional dual-income couple, but much has changed, as the finance industry had to extend its appeal to a broader base of customers.

As we stated at the start of this chapter, the binary between male and female, feminine and masculine, runs through our culture. In popular discourse, the assumption is that these divisions are natural and biologically formed, but we now understand that both sexuality and gender roles are socially constructed and performed across various settings, including the home (Irigaray, 1985). Subjectivities in relation to sexuality are actualized through socialization, beginning in childhood. Young children acquire an understanding of sexuality and gender roles through their interactions in the home (primarily with parent(s) and siblings). As they grow older, it is common for children to avoid talking to their parents directly about sexuality and to further their knowledge from socialization at school and through peers and media (Robinson, Hockey, and Meah, 2004; Gorman-Murray, 2012). In part, this reticence by parents and children is attributable perhaps to the way sexuality is portrayed in contemporary culture.

For children, sexuality is learned partially in the home from their parents, but learning also comes from their friends and at school. Increasingly, knowledge and understanding of sexuality is acquired through the Internet and popular culture. Sexuality is a complex negotiation in which boundaries are being pushed, choices made, and accommodations enacted. As Gorman-Murray argues, the ideals associated with both male and female are enacted in the home space, and this helps explain how the prototype suburban home is associated with nuclear families. However, these ideals are constantly under threat from societal changes. To supply an obvious example, the liberalization of sexual practices commencing in the 1960s and the subsequent commercialization of sex through media, such as the Internet and TV, have generated further shifts in sexual practices and attitudes. Sex is increasingly associated with leisure rather than reproduction, and this is clearly to be seen in the proliferation of domestic sex work and the demand for such services. Suburban homes are increasingly being used as places for sex work, rendering the traditional assumptions about sex work being primarily a nighttime and largely inner-city phenomenon increasingly redundant (Bell and Valentine, 1995).

Any discussion of identity and sexuality requires an acknowledgment of the caring role enacted within homes spaces. The dominant binary of male and female is enacted discursively in the spaces of home. Traditionally, it is the male (father) who usually occupies the symbolic and formal position of breadwinner, and it is mothers who act as carers and homemakers. Heteronormativity establishes a set of roles for couples and children. However, there have been significant changes over the last forty years, and coming out as gay or transgender is likely to meet less consternation from parents than before, although it is far from easy. In nontraditional nuclear households (single parents, queer couples, transgender partners, and so on), different constructions of sexuality are enacted, but contemporary societies often remain a place where the home still performs as an imagined site for heterosexual couples to live in domestic bliss. The ideal of the home as a place to "settle down and bring up a family" retains a hold on popular culture. We see that care within the household and a sense of obligation makes kin and non-kin "feel at home." When we live in a house where care is withdrawn, we feel unease, and our dwelling ceases to feel like "home."

As housing becomes more expensive and where elderly people choose not to live in nursing homes, the work of caring for elderly parents is often informally assumed by children. Intergenerational care in the home for elderly relatives has increased, and many young children have to adopt informal caring roles in contemporary Britain for sick or disabled family members. Bowlby, McKie, Gregory, and McPherson (2010) have argued that obligations of care often leave women feeling tied and suffering from a lack of privacy vis-à-vis other household members. The absence of such care is often now understood not only as neglect but also as a form of abuse.

It should be apparent that sexuality cannot be easily defined or entirely attributable to notions of gender. Instead, it is a form of sociality that is subject to societal changes. This noted, we can state with confidence that elements of sexuality in the home exhibit tensions and contradictions that are carefully kept from public view. Despite the changes in sexual practices and the more open attitudes toward nontraditional relationships, the home retains its power as an imaginary for conventional forms of heteronormativity. The meaning and significance of home is to some extent shaped by our attitudes toward love, caring, and sexuality. Our fraught attitudes regarding sexuality partially explain our ambiguous relationship with home. It is a place that is sanctuary, but also at times an intimate but conflicted space in which we forge our notions of selfhood.

Exercises

1. Is there such a thing as a typical home?
2. To what extent is gender enacted and shaped as a result of the physical layout of the home?
3. Is there such a thing as a heterosexual or gay home? Again, how does the physical structure reflect sexual desires?
4. What are the differences among household, dwelling, and family? To what extent do our norms about relationships and social units shape these definitions? To what extent does the physical structure of the home shape the possibility of certain kinds of household? Discuss using the examples of flats, huts, and large suburban homes.

Conclusion

What takes place in the home, the relationships, the encounters with objects, and the practices of self-formation can all be interpreted by different sociological lenses. Marxist interpretations emphasize the role of home in the processes of capital accumulation. Through this lens, the home performs to meet the needs of capitalist production. Homes are constructed as places of leisure and rest as a way to assuage our concerns about exploitation in the world of work. Feminist perspectives see homemaking through the prism of patriarchy. From this vista, the home is where exploitation takes place in a myriad of forms, domestic violence being its most extreme variant, but also in unacknowledged emotional and care work largely undertaken by females in the home.

Finally, some mention should be made of some other currently influential perspectives. The actor network theories associated with Bruno Latour (1993) position the home as a site of material practices in which both human and non-humans generate effects. According to this view, the material and the social is one and the same: plants, pets, and devices such as washing machines, microwaves, TVs, computers, kitchen sinks, and furniture are entangled. The home and the world are mixtures of human and non-human material artifacts, nature, and culture (see Shove et al., 2007, for a discussion on how non-human artifacts interact and shape the way we inhabit the home and transform long-established dynamics among its members).

5 The Loss of Home

Introduction

The destruction or loss of the home is one of the most significant and damaging crises within the range of human experience. The severed connections to the house as a physical space, to shelter, nurture, and enable social interaction, generate a range of emotional and physical responses, from feelings of trauma, vulnerability, and anger, to a sense of mourning that may endure for years after the event. Sociologists have also helped to chart the range of dramatic and direct health impacts on those sleeping rough (outside, on the street, with little or no shelter or protection) or those living with friends and relatives. There are many routes to lost homes, and such experiences are by no means restricted only to the poor and excluded. Forced evictions, foreclosures, homelessness, natural disasters (interacting with human-made problems like the inadequate quality of housing to withstand earthquakes) or the bombing and destruction of homes in wartime conditions are among an array of displacing forces that go well beyond ordinary household mobility and the choice to move home. Many of these processes are deeply located within broader patterns and structures of power, inequality, and legal strictures that may mandate and uphold forced removal from the home, despite being deeply resented by the owner or tenant of a dwelling. Losing a home highlights how embedded and connected we are to our personal assets that we cherish, maintain, and develop relationships with, often over many years and in conjunction with friends, family, and social connections in the area.

In this chapter, we consider the various routes by which homes are lost and examine the social forces, geographies, and inequalities that accentuate these problems. Many households and individuals leave their homes not because they want to do so, but because they are compelled by a range of complex forces. We consider the social causes and impacts of these processes and various kinds of social and economic power, as well as the direct use of force that requires people to abandon their homes. The loss of domestic homes often occurs neither as a random or occasional event, but as frequent tragedies that are structured and propelled by national and global economy and political structures, including the withdrawal of financial support to the vulnerable, the turbulence of the global economy, and use of military force. As social scientists, we must be alert to the human consequences of such tragedies, but, more importantly, we should also question how the structural workings of economies and political systems influence the shape and extent of such experiences on the ground in social geographies and social groups most often subjected to these forms of loss and the effects of that loss on them. In Chapter 9, we will return to issues of gentrification and the way that it has displaced households by raising house prices and rents in many neighborhoods around the world.

The many ways of losing a home

Destruction—demolition
Eviction—public and private housing
Harassment—by landlords or agents of the state
Megaproject construction—dams or stadiums
Displacement—being priced-out through the unregulated operation
 of the housing market
Catastrophe—fire, flood, earthquake, tsunami
Warfare—bombardment, razing

The political economy of the loss of home

However it occurs, for many households the loss of the home is a personal disaster on many levels, but we must also consider how these forms of emotional damage and human distress are generated by larger systemic forces and processes. We underscore here that the world system is a conceptual framework to account for the ways that national and supranational societies and economies privilege key actors and nations over time. The foremost scholar of world system theory is Immanuel Wallerstein (1999). He argues that the modern state is best understood in the wider context of a world system, and this is necessary if we are to ascertain the social divisions and conflicts that persist over time. For Wallerstein, capitalist markets feature inherent contradictions that lead to damaging consequences for particular localities and for vulnerable social groups within them.

Wallerstein's work has been influential and served as an example for other academics to contextualize the nation-state in a broader setting, such as the Marxist inspired Göran Therborn (2013), who argues that capitalist societies are configured in ways that serve the interests of elites and ensure that they remain in privileged positions. Electoral democracies amplify this need for growth, to enable structurally positioned elites and affluent socioeconomic classes to do well, and to reproduce these positions over time by offering tax and other advantages (such as an ambition to produce low interest rates for homeowners) to those who vote in support of them and to those who occupy positions of social, economic, and political power. Often referred to as "political economy," many analysts of global and economic conditions seek to understand how decisions concerning how many houses to build, what kind of economy to seek to build, and who benefits most from economic growth and activity are not neutral decisions, but operate within a complex matrix of positions, actors, institutions, and interests. It is those with greater money, power, electoral clout, or historically vested interests and established positions that do best. Governments seek to publicize their policies in ways that are appealing and popular, but this should not lull us into accepting their activities as benevolent. A more prescient understanding is one that recognizes how governments are influenced by powerful vested interests that often work behind the scenes to ensure their interests are maintained.

The long-run consequences of inequality and political life involve the story of housing development and owner occupation in interesting ways. In preceding chapters, we noted how David Harvey (1976, 2010) has long argued that urban land markets exhibit patterns of investment and systems of generating profitability for wealthy groups. More recently, he argued that suburbanization also played a major strategic role in accumulation for capitalist systems while generating immense areas of urban sprawl and new possibilities for crises. Perhaps one of the most important contributions to these more recent debates has been offered by Saskia Sassen (2014), who developed the idea of displacement and exclusion into an analysis of different forms of human expulsion that now operate globally. For Sassen, ideas of exclusion do not fully encompass the ways in which housing, land, political, and economic systems are increasingly designed or operate in ways that propel people from homes and land in dramatic and socially unjust ways. These are important contextual issues in detailing and understanding the geography and social groups most affected by the loss of home, as we shall see.

The main point to take from such observations by Wallerstein, Harvey, and others is that critical approaches to the broader constitution and operation of our economic systems, expressed, for example, through systems of trade in the housing market, do not operate in a social and political vacuum. Instead, they are critically located within the decisions of important political actors and parties with interests aligned with and supported by investment capital, the wealthy, and homeowners. This means that not only do housing inequalities reflect and reinforce the winners and losers of capitalist societies but also that such outcomes are further reinforced through flows of money in housing markets and the way that they create tenurial, class, and wealth-based inequalities.

Writers like Harvey have made detailed, critical arguments about how the capitalist system itself has been sustained by construction projects via the expansion of the suburbs in the postwar/mid-twentieth-century period. For Harvey, such projects enabled accumulated capital to work by investing in massive construction projects used to generate further capital. As capital became over-accumulated in the built environment, and with too much development threatened by other economic crises, the risk of a financial crash not only became more apparent, but was also linked to lending practices to vulnerable "at-risk" households because banks and finance organizations sought potential rewards by lending money to them at high rates of return. Both the construction of the American residential and urban landscape (see, e.g., Warner, 1978, or Hayden, 2009), and the attempt to expand home ownership thereby became important forms of expansion, risk, and economic recessions over the postwar period.

For Harvey, these changes are explicable by reference to the deeper structures of the capitalist economy prone to these forms of expansion and contraction. For writers like Dorling (2014) and Lanchester (2010), the international system of housing finance and the extension of complex financial instruments is testimony to the way that housing is central to the operations of international capital. According to Lanchester (2010), it was ultimately the inability to locate riskier mortgage debts within bigger bundles of debt that were being bought and sold for profit by these institutions that led to the massive loss of confidence and subsequent global economic reverse. We now understand that the irony of this systemic crisis was the extension of much greater levels of risk to poorer and more precariously employed owners caught up in a wave of repossession activity that featured in 2008. To date, these foreclosures have sent more than 7 million US households into the hands of their lenders, and around another half million are currently in some stage of foreclosure (CoreLogic, 2015). The domino effect of the crisis gave rise to so-called austerity government programs that have further accentuated levels of unemployment, economic stagnation, and the defunding of public welfare. These impacts have undoubtedly increased the risk of households becoming homeless (see below).

Faced with global capitalism and its systemic foundation upon the desire and promotion of increasing rates of economic growth and profitability, we can make a number of assertions in relation to the housing system relevant to how people may end up losing their homes. First, housing has become a fundamental aspect of capitalist economies and strategies for growing wealth among these societies' elites. This works in multiple ways, primarily through offering incentives for people to realize home ownership, but it also harnesses households to long periods of increasingly intense indebtedness, placing them at risk of losing their homes when other aspects of their economic life (during work, or in old age and retirement, despite the possibility that their mortgage debts may have been paid off by this time) become unstable. Second, housing and the economy are increasingly tied to political projects in important ways that may have impact on the relative vulnerability of low-income households. Attempts at generating national economic growth have often been attached to the remaking of urban centers and have involved the demolition of homes in cities across the world, a kind of creative-destructive force that has affected the lives of many millions globally (Davis, 2006). For example, the Beijing Olympic Games involved the demolition of more than a million homes in order to promote the city and develop infrastructure, and in Rio de Janeiro, slum areas are increasingly commodified and made available for sale as the wider property market and house prices have heated up. In cities like Rio, the theoretical designs of writers like Neil Smith (1979, 2005) appear prescient, highlighting how disinvestment and poor economic conditions ultimately generate areas ripe for investment—cheaper areas and homes that can be appropriated, renovated, and sold for a profit involving wider processes of gentrification. These forms of speculative investment operate unbounded across national boundaries, with important effects. One notable effect of the expansion of capital flows has been for property lenders and banks to operate in new regions globally and to take advantage of newly commodifying state housing resources.

Smith and LeFaivre (1984) have argued that "capitalism is based precisely on its ability to displace the working class in all sorts of situations, and history has shown us many examples of the ways in which legislatures, the wealthy, and the politically influential have managed to move the poor when it was profitable or expedient to do so." There is a very long history to such processes; the clearance of the Scottish Highlands, the development of the railways, slum clearance programs, and housing grants all led to large sections of the population, inevitably the poorest, being displaced. What these processes have in common is that they affect those groups who have the least capacity to resist. Speculative investment in housing inevitably reduces the security of those with the quietest political voice and least wealth (see LeGates and Hartman, 1986).

Homelessness

Now that we have established the wider economic and social processes that shape housing, in this section we narrow our focus to consider how homelessness is both experienced and managed by policy makers. As social inequality intensifies, incidences of homelessness will become more prevalent and enduring. As a long-standing social problem, it has generated significant interest from social researchers. The question of what counts as being homeless is a critical problem in its own right. Many people traditionally think of homelessness in terms of people sleeping rough. This is only one manifestation of the problem. Homelessness covers unfit habitation of various sorts: people finding shelter in derelict buildings, squatting, living permanently in structures designed for short-term use only, caravans, tents—the list goes on. Importantly, it is equally possible to be without one's own home and live by "sofa surfing," sleeping on people's floors or empty spaces. A key point to make here is that homelessness tends to be defined restrictively by those on the political right so that responses are only considered for those sleeping rough, for example (Jacobs, Kemeny, and Manzi, 1999). The social roots of homelessness are complex and often interlinked. In this section, we offer an overview of the complexities of defining this social phenomenon and how researchers have understood the social causes and kinds of impacts that homelessness generates for those it touches.

Particularly in the media, it is not uncommon to frame homelessness as a pathological issue, the attribution of victims as somehow being culpable for their own predicament because of personal failings. This view of homelessness is popular among conservative-minded policymakers as it provides a rationale to reduce the scope and cost of government intervention. As we have suggested, a more insightful way to understand the causes of homelessness is to see it as a symptom of social inequality and the lack of public housing. This noted, there are other factors that can lead individuals to homelessness, such as long-term drug and alcohol addiction, time in prison, or flight from persecution, in the case of some migrants.

In the poorest nation-states, homeless populations live in informal settlements where there is also little or no acknowledgment of homelessness. This is also often linked to the lack of development of welfare duties by governments as well as the poverty of many people living in these countries. In India and China, around 50,000 households are accepted each year as homeless; however, close to double this number apply for a home. The scale of this problem is clearly much deeper in Mexico City. There are estimates of as many as 1.5 million children living on the streets in the capital (Jones and De Benitez, 2012). In some of the poorest regions of the world, it is certainly difficult to quantify the homeless. What we do know is that it is in the poorest regions where people who are street-homeless are most vulnerable to the elements and to attacks or abuse from other people on the streets. It is here that government agencies lack the resources to forge a strategy or are of such a political disposition that they seek not to acknowledge or assist.

We end our brief discussion of homelessness by looking at the impact of natural disaster and its interplay with regional economic and social conditions that amplify these problems. The challenges of addressing homelessness are all the more formidable when natural disasters take place. In the period following earthquakes or floods, it is not unusual for many people to seek refuge in large transitory settlements that rely on governmental and charitable support. Research undertaken in the aftermath of Hurricane Katrina demonstrated that it is the poorest households who are often the most vulnerable during natural disasters (Elliot and Pais, 2006). These households are less likely to have financial resources to meet the costs of damage to their property and often live in low-lying areas that are more vulnerable to flooding.

Among the conclusions we can draw from this discussion is that homelessness is a symptom of social inequality, and its prevalence reflects the intensification of inequality in the current era of neoliberalism. Where they occur, government interventions mostly target individual assistance rather than addressing the supply-side shortages that lead to homelessness. In the current era of austerity expenditure, it is difficult to foresee any major significant shift in policies dealing with this problem.

Gentrification and household displacement: Being priced out

Homelessness is the most extreme symptom of social inequality in the context of housing, but what other symptoms can we observe? In the concluding section of this chapter, we return to the discussion of gentrification (further discussed in Chapter 9). As discussed there, gentrification refers to a process in which higher-income households move to and invest in more deprived or working-class urban and rural areas. This process of renewal tends to mask a problematic aspect of such changes in the form of pressures on tenants in these areas, who are often compelled to leave through eviction or being priced out of their properties through rent increases. It is also possible for owners to be displaced by gentrification if, in some jurisdictions, property taxes are increased. Displacement from gentrification forces the loss of a home upon those with low incomes and often those from minority ethnic populations (Atkinson 2000a, 2000b, and 2002). Of course, gentrification may not necessarily displace anyone at all; people may migrate by choice rather than force or economic necessity. Yet these social choices may still generate problematic economic consequences as "price shadowing" occurs in relation to the rents and prices of properties nearby, which may create pressures on those with fewer resources. Similarly, major changes in labor markets—the closure of factories, for example— may force households and workers to relocate to find new opportunities.

Gentrification appears to improve the physical and social fabric of an area while appealing to the activities of profit-making investment in run-down areas. The process also appeals to a logic within the market allocation of housing resources; in some cities and neighborhoods, we find that poorer areas are seen as problematic, and the kind of physical and social changes that occur in tandem with gentrification may make them appealing to others. Such arguments form one side of a coin, the flip side of which is that social problems are essentially evacuated (e.g., the argument that gentrification simply reduces crime) through the "improvement" of neighborhoods and are thereby used as evidence that gentrification has positive impacts on social problems, such as the reduction of crime or improvement of commercial services. Such a view is giving way to an awareness that it is relative social diversity and not homogeneous environments, be they rich or poor, which are most successful at reducing neighborhood problems (Atkinson and Kintrea, 2001).

Gentrification is now widespread globally (Smith, 1995), and so are pressures of displacement. Housing changes through gentrification in many US, Australian, European, and other cities globally mean that hundreds of thousands have been displaced. Extensive research has been conducted in North America, where displacement has been defined as occurring when "any household is forced to move from its residence by conditions which affect the dwelling or its immediate surroundings" (US Department of Housing and Urban Development in LeGates and Hartman, 1986: 214). The housing sociologist Peter Marcuse (1986) identified four types of displacement: economic/physical (where residents are priced out of a dwelling through rent increases or by physical means); last resident displacement (only the last resident is counted as displaced); chain displacement (counting includes the number of residents over time which have been displaced from a property); and finally, exclusionary displacement (a figure which includes those who have been unable to access property because it has been gentrified, yet who have some connection to the area). These definitions are important in considering the extent of displacement, its social effects, and how to respond to this problem.

Levels of displacement have been a contentious issue. In the United States, Sumka estimated that 500,000 households, roughly 2 million people, were displaced annually (Sumka, 1979). LeGates and Hartman (1986) viewed this as a purposeful undercount by the Department of Housing and Urban Development. LeGates and Hartman estimated that at least a further half million people displaced annually would be both an "approximate and conservative measure." Yet separating gentrification and displacement from wider processes of social and urban change, we see that incumbent upgrading (residents in area improving their own social conditions over time), voluntary migration and welfare, and labor market changes create obstacles for measuring such processes. Further, it is exceedingly hard to distinguish between gentrification as a form of neighborhood replacement or displacement. Although cities like London have been the focus of increasing polarization and occupational restructuring (Hamnett, 2003), little work has been done on displacement. Early studies often found that many tenants moved due to landlord harassment and these problems find echoes with processes of public housing demolitions and evictions in London at this time, and the gentrification and displacement of many areas in cities like San Francisco and Berlin or Melbourne and Sydney (Atkinson, 2015).

Demolition and privatization

Finally, it is important to consider the impact on disadvantaged households of slum clearance. The term *community displacement* has been used to describe the outcomes for many households who have lived in neighborhoods that have undergone "regeneration" (see, e.g., Shaw and Hagemans's 2015 case study of inner Melbourne). Community displacements are a feature of other redevelopment programs such as building large road projects or new, large sports stadiums.

Over the last few years, demolition has been an issue for urban regions outside the South East of England, and much of it has concerned council or former council estates. Earlier research estimated that only a tiny fraction (around 1%) of all council housing was demolished in the period 1991–97 but that the pace of demolitions was on the increase. Since then, demolition has been used to assist in city restructuring programs to adjust to low demand, as well as to promote a so-called "urban renaissance" project. It is also a feature of refinancing initiatives for council housing such as stock transfer to registered social landlords (RSLs) and private finance initiative (PFI) schemes (Raco, 2013). In the early 1990s, stock transfer affected mostly unproblematic housing, but now it has extended to major urban areas with concentrations of obsolete and unpopular housing. For example, Glasgow's stock transfer proposals entail clearing 11,000 homes. Clearance is also a feature for older, privately owned, "inner-city" areas, especially in the north of England, where the market has broadly failed to generate the right kind and quality of housing.

During and after the great postwar era of slum clearance that peaked about 1970, researchers and other writers were diligent in investigating the administrative competence and social impact of slum clearance. Early studies tended to concentrate on impacts on social life, whereas later accounts were much more critical of the administrative process (Heywood and Naz, 1990). The key point for many of these researchers concerned the lack of consultation and disempowerment of the residents of areas affected, and even more importantly, the way their social networks and support mechanisms were broken or damaged by being compelled to move to new neighborhoods. Although many or even most residents approved of clearance, the studies variously reached these conclusions:

- The declaration of clearance areas led to "planning blight" and made bad social and physical conditions even worse.
- Life in clearance areas was very difficult for residents, who had to cope with disrepair, poor or missing services, and the breakup of their communities.
- Time scales for clearance were often unspecific, leading to years of uncertainty.
- The process was bureaucratic and fragmented; there was often no consultation and little information, and authorities were high-handed and paternalistic.

- Residents were often left ill-informed and confused.
- The process had ill effects on some people's mental health.
- Offers of rehousing were often made on subjective and judgmental grounds, and the outcomes were unfair and even racist.
- Homeowners tied up in the process were often inadequately compensated for home loss.
- Re-housing often isolated people from the social networks on which they relied for survival.

Housing clearance continues, but there is a paucity of research on good practice in the clearance process and assessment of the social outcomes. Although problems endure, lessons were learned from the experiences of the 1970s. For example, most councils have sought to encourage resident involvement, and the scale of demolition is generally much smaller in comparison to the comprehensive redevelopment of inner-city districts in the 1960s and early 1970s. However, in the current redevelopment programs, residents are relatively more disadvantaged and vulnerable compared to their 1970s counterparts, occupying the least desirable homes in a residualized social housing sector.

The intentional destruction of the home: Domicide

It is one thing to lose a home because of the pressures of cost or the actions of the state or markets, but it is also possible that homes are destroyed purposefully in order to displace whole populations or groups occupying particular homes and regions. The term *domicide* was coined by Douglas Porteous and Sandra Smith (2001) to capture such processes. They used the term to refer to the "deliberate destruction of home by human agency in pursuit of specified goals, which causes suffering to the victims" (p. 12). Acts such as dam construction or urban redevelopment have often involved large-scale and compulsory destruction of poor people's homes. In addition, many of the most extreme events in social history, such as war and ethnic cleansing, have led to the destruction of homes and the expulsion of large populations, both within and across national boundaries.

Although the home is often considered the core social space, protected by property laws, it is also overlaid with significant variations in tenurial security, by the varying incomes and circumstances of the inhabiting household and by broader social, political, and economic forces that may serve to undermine or finally destroy the links between dweller and dwelling. Because home expresses significant aspects of affective development, identity formation, and physical and income security, the idea of domicide presents us with a concept through which we can explore the destruction and loss of a foundational aspect of our broader social lives. Understanding the depth and nature of such a relationship is critical to a subsequent comprehension of the immiseration generated by such destruction and the urgency of projects by which such aggression might be halted. Continued wartime conflict, such as the civil war in Syria or the development of megaprojects (such as dam, airport, and road construction), and the restructuring of urban fabrics through processes of demolition in many urban centers, globally continue to make the concept of domicide a useful term.

Porteous and Smith (2001) distinguished between two forms of domicide: the extreme and the everyday. Their intention here was to delineate between irregular and extensive acts of domestic destruction (extreme), such as that generated through war, from those woven into the daily patterns of capitalist, urban political economy and property relations (the everyday), such as compulsory purchase and neighborhood renewal. Under the former, they include the examples of South Africa's Bantustans, where 15 million black people were concentrated within 13% of the nation's land, and Israel's forced displacement of around a million Palestinian households, along with the physical destruction of many homes and villages. It also includes widespread dam building projects that have generated the displacement of up to 80 million households, globally.

Domicide brings into the housing researcher's lexicon the theaters of war, human aggression, and the destructive elements of everyday life in most regions of the globe. It sets conventional and often Western notions of tacitly understood perpetuity and the stability of domestic life against such threats. Capitalist land relations, the power and expansion of corporate commodity extraction, and major income inequalities act as the fertile ground upon which domicide is permitted or carried out by political and industrial elites. Embedded, continued warfare and civic strife in many regions highlight how domicide continues with depressing regularity, often used as revenge in ethnic conflicts or deemed in the interests of the greater good in the context of many development projects.

Recent figures on the scale of domicide can be determined to some extent via the reports of the United Nation's High Commissioner for Refugees (UNHCR). Their latest report (UNHCR, 2014) concluded that there were 59.5 million people forcibly displaced and that this figure included 19.5 million refugees (though it is not clear how many of these people's homes were destroyed, and therefore it is not clear what proportion can be considered linked acts of domicide in the strict sense). The UNHCR offered protection or assistance to 25 million such people. The United Nations Office for the Coordination of Humanitarian Affairs (UNOCHA) also estimated an *additional* 25 million people have been displaced due to natural disasters (*Forced Migration Review 20*, 2004). This brings in a related but conceptually distinct process: the un-housing of people through such catastrophes.

Porteous and Smith note that many of those affected by domicide remain internally displaced in the countries they come from. Figures for 2009 from the International Committee of the Red Cross estimate that there are 26 million internally displaced people globally, casualties of war who feel the terror of possible or actual attack on homelands and dwellings. The Red Cross cites the use of starvation, attacks on civilian sites, and the obstruction of relief as key tactics driving these human flows, often to informal or "containment camps" run by agencies like the Red Cross itself. As a representative example, they suggest that 40,000 internally displaced people were generated by the Israeli war in Lebanon, 2007. To these enormous tolls, the same report adds a further 25 million people generated by natural disaster and a further final 11.4 million international refugees.

The United Nations noted dramatic increases in these figures over time, with ongoing violence in countries like Iraq (which has generated the greatest number of refugees [2.2 million]) and Afghanistan (1.9 million; UN estimates for 2007). As far back as 2000 there were still 7 million Palestinian refugees in the world, many seeking a right to return to settlements (after fleeing the war of 1948) systematically destroyed in the space that became Israel.

Data issues clearly remain a challenge; many refugees have not suffered domicide in the strict sense of the word intended by Porteous and Smith. Refugees are easier to monitor and catalog, whereas the internally displaced are harder to categorize, are not considered legal refugees by the UN, and so do not qualify for aid. Not all refugees will be led to seek shelter as a result of the actual destruction of their homes, and yet their continued existence and sustenance within the dwelling has been made impossible, often because their sociopolitical lives have been compromised.

Some researchers have gathered estimates relating to the domicide of homes to enable (often Western-funded) megaprojects. According to those findings, 4–80 million people have been displaced by dam construction. In early 2007, the BBC reported that the Chinese Three Gorges Dam project would displace around 1.4 million people, but shortly after, the UK *Guardian* newspaper detailed plans for a further 4 million people to be moved from their homes to ensure the "environmental safety" of the dam, one of the biggest resettlements in modern history. Ironically, at least one rationale for the dam is to reduce China's reliance on coal-fired power stations, themselves part of a broader conflagration of forces generating the climate change that has made settlements on the steeply sided areas adjacent to the dam more vulnerable to mud slides.

The plight of Arabs in Southern Iraq reveals a prime example of the destruction of homeland linked to domicide. It was here that Saddam Hussein drained the marshes, creating one of the first groups to be recognized as environmental refugees. Estimates of the number of Arabs displaced by these acts vary significantly, from around 40,000 to 1,000,000. Domicide also relates to the relationship among informal settlements, tenure, and questions of national sovereignty and migration. This complex amalgam was raised in the destruction of the "jungle" camp close to the channel tunnel, where those already displaced from countries like Afghanistan and Iraq saw the French state dismantle their temporary homes, leading to a second round of homelessness and dispossession from the meager, tentative grasp on shelter they were able to manage.

In countries like the United Kingdom, the postwar period was marked by a move to rehabilitate and clear many sections of bomb-damaged and blighted urban areas, often built according to poor standards by private developers in earlier decades. The slum clearance of this period moved many tens of thousands of households, particularly in the larger cities, such as London, Birmingham, and Glasgow. In the name of the common good, many people were moved to areas of new public housing to improve their conditions and health. Such programs, given the grieving for social systems of support documented in books like Young and Wilmott's *Family and Kinship in East London*, highlighted an often-misguided policy that generated many secondary problems. Calling such policies acts of domicide would no doubt generate significant debate given the deep and genuine problems of these areas. Older examples of domicide abound and include the Scottish Highland clearances, the complex relationships among land, economy, and ethnicity that resulted in the potato famine in Ireland, and even the re-siting of smaller English villages within country estates, often carried out to improve the views of the landed gentry. Current policies in the United Kingdom and the United States to assist housing markets by governments have raised these problems again. Such programs continue to raise questions about the way that public policy has periodically compelled people to leave their homes when they have not wanted to.

Domicide can be seen as a subset of complex forces that generate the loss of home. Such loss may be generated by a range of sources. Porteous and Smith concern themselves with the misery and victimization generated by the intentional destruction of home. Many studies of such phenomena have been carried out, such as those on dam building, indigenous peoples, the impact of war, and the like. It is not clear whether the concept requires or would benefit from refinement to encompass other processes through which the home is lost or whether destruction of the home and human intentionality should be considered its hallmarks.

Climate change has also been responsible for the significant destruction of homelands, and more directly, property, such as that seen in the aftermath of Hurricane Katrina in New Orleans and the social geography of its impacts on the city's black population. Similarly, the broader impacts of catastrophes, like the tsunami of 2007, highlight the interplay of social geography and national and social inequalities that mediate and amplify the effects of such disasters.

Exercises

1. What can sociologists contribute to debates about what is to be done to prevent the loss of the home? Consider this in relation to the issues of gentrification and displacement in the global North and that of slum clearance and domicide in the Global South.
2. What are the primary social, economic, and political drivers of the loss of people's homes?

Conclusion

We have covered a wide range of topics in this chapter, but there are some important conclusions we can reach. Studies of housing in the global West have often focused on socioeconomic, problem-based questions, such as affordability, quality, and supply among many others. For sociologists eager to analyze some of the most forceful and difficult housing problems, the loss of home emerges as foremost of these concerns. We have argued that patterns and processes of homelessness, domicide, and the clearance and demolition of homes can be linked to national economic and political forms of power, enabled by forms of housing law that privilege the wealthy. These are not the only ways households are displaced. The process of displacement has also been responsible for large amounts of household misery, moving tenants and others from homes and neighborhoods to which they have deep attachments. The net impact of these various forms of loss is incredibly difficult to calculate, despite the brave attempts of international agencies, some governments, and academic researchers. The scale of these issues is often so great as to seem intractable. Certainly without systemic changes to reduce inequalities, reframing tenant law, and enabling the rights of those in homes to stay put, many acts of displacement will continue to affect poor and politically excluded groups.

6

Domestic Criminology: Crime, Harm and Victimization in the Home

Introduction

In this chapter, criminology is considered through the lens of the domestic home. Criminology is the study of the reasons for crime and harm and our responses to these problems and is identified with sociological efforts at understanding the kinds of social structures that generate violence and harm against others (Cohen, 1988). As we have already argued, the predominant association of the private home is with a space of safety and refuge, yet it is also a place of fear and violence, more often from others within the household than from without (burglary and invasion). The home is one of the primary sites of physical violence and a place where long-running, deep, psychic injuries occur, often focused around gender relations and household conflict. And although the private home is culturally positioned as a place of intrinsic social goodness, shelter, and personal autonomy, it is simultaneously the locus of widely shared emotions—fear, increasing social precariousness, what sociologists call ontological insecurity—the sense that the very world around us is unpredictable and a threat. From inside our homes we look outward, measuring the dangerous world outside through its windows and the portals of our increasingly complex media systems. Our goal here is to provide an account of the ways the physical shell of the home and the soft social life of its interior connect to our understanding of these problems.

In the United States and Australia each year, about one-third of all violent crimes occur in or near the private home, whereas the British Crime Survey (BCS) (Walker, Flatley, Kershaw, and Moon, 2009) suggests that around 13% of women and 9% of men have been subject to domestic violence (abuse, threats, or force), sexual victimization, or stalking in the past twelve months. The private home is a prime location for acts of violence, but is also a site in which violence may be reproduced through the socialization and generation of violent or criminal social actors. Yet the home itself is not a standardized product, nor does it provide a uniform series of social experiences; the home is a space of personal development and a space in which relative propensities to transgress social rules may be shaped in part within family life.

The inequality that has grown so dramatically in Western societies over the past four decades has not only driven many of the harms that criminologists monitor (Currie, 2009; Young, 2007), but such polarization has also led to varied social outcomes in and outside the home. How we treat children, the quality and assuredness of family and kin supports, the availability of communal and state provision, and the broader economic circumstances that allow us (or not) to "make" a home are phenomena that are central to understanding the forces that shape criminal and harmful acts. The home is central, but often neglected, in criminology; this is in part because what goes on in the home has tended to be private, a space out of bounds to many researchers, and the experience of domestic violence has also been generally underreported and fraught with a gender politics that sometimes contests findings.

The home is also important because, as social scientists are increasingly aware, space matters (Tickamyer, 2000). The patterning of people and groups in urban spaces and in particular homes and tenures is important in shaping opportunities and constraints, as well as the relative stresses and internal social controls that shape deviant conduct or predatory behavior. Neighborhoods, estates, and blocks speak to us symbolically of the inequities and problems of our societies and also of social boundaries and various borders offering buffers against harm in some locations. Whether we own our own home or not is a crude but effective indicator of wealth, safety from intrusion, the deployment of domestic security systems, or reduced worry about crime; by extension, lives lived in rented housing tend to highlight the converse. Consider burglary, a phenomenon that generates anxiety, fear, and also considerable anger where and when it occurs. The experience of burglary is not a general problem across social space. The risk of victimization varies considerably, according to pertinent characteristics of the household and area. For example, in the Crime Survey for England and Wales, households in areas where physical disorder, such as areas of graffiti, physical damage to property, and so on, was assessed as high were more likely to be victims of burglary (5.1%) than those in areas where the assessed level was not high (2.2%). Similarly, more affluent households and those who actually own their own homes have both the resources and incentives that are found much less often among poor owners and private renters to secure their homes. Thus, a patchwork of risks, insecurities, and harms can be identified between the home itself and the wider sociospatial context of individual homes. It is to this connection that this chapter is devoted.

Housing studies and studies of crime

Despite easily recognizable impressions of the primary locus of much crime, criminologists have not seen the domestic home as a site of particular interest in its own right (though questions of environmental criminology, where crime happens, and why, have often made reference to the design and architecture of homes; more detail on these issues appears in Chapter 10). There are many ways to assert the value of the home in discussions of crime and social harm. Many of them are explicit in criminological thinking, such as domestic violence. Others are yet to be adequately explored, such as the rise of what might called fortress homes (Atkinson and Blandy, 2007) or the role of housing policy in producing concentrated social desolation and vulnerability (Flint and Nixon, 2006). We can also think of the home as a site of social control, as a defense mechanism against harm, and as a space nested within other spatial, social, and political contexts.

Criminological interest in houses and homes can be split into three components or meanings: as a site within a number of key contexts; as a physical dwelling or object that has particular construction and architectural qualities; and as a site of crime, harm, and fear. The first concern, the context of the home, is clearly important. This refers to the various social, political, and economic contexts outside the home but which act upon its constitution or the variability of outcomes within. The main agent here is the state, varying macroeconomic policies that generate homes of particular qualities and standards (consider the impact of the deregulation of sound insulation standards on levels of aggression and claims of antisocial behavior in many new-build "executive" flats today). The housing system is also a crucial sphere within which inequalities are born and reproduced. Winners and losers emerge from a private market in housing while a socially residualized public housing system caters to the worst off. In Britain, the state and its myriad offshoots regulate space and citizens via housing associations and an array of policing measures that have emerged in the past twenty years that also contribute to attempts to control antisocial and disorderly populations in areas left behind in the move to a new economy.

What happens in these broad sociopolitical and economic contexts outside the home also shapes experiences inside. Watchful owners take shelter from disorder and dangers generated by systemic inequalities; cultural attitudes around gender roles shape private experiences of abuse; and economic systems and politically driven resource allocations generate unequal access to safe housing. These various forces and factors, linking the micro-society of domestic space to social forces and spatial contexts outside the front door, bedroom window, or Internet terminal, are critical to a domestic criminology. Among other areas, debates about fear of crime implicitly locate the social subject indoors, looking out upon possible risks or worrisome events. More deeply, a political economy that directs allocations to affluent homeowners generates a set of economic winners and losers that meshes with class systems and affects our exposure to particular kinds of risk and our capacity to avoid harms. Among such patterns is not least the use of home search strategies that are elaborate avoidance techniques and which result in the critical concentration of those *with* resources in spaces set against and as far as possible away from those *without*.

Dwellings are highly varied in their design, defensive capacities, and spatial configuration. This is well evidenced in concerns about target hardening, which portrays home as an object seen as being amenable to adaptation to reduce the risk from those seeking targets for vandalism or entry. Newman's (1972) work in this field was a bold attempt to protect public housing tenants identified as vulnerable and living in embattled conditions during the long rise of violent crime in the 1960s and 1970s. As work on burglary and target-hardening has shown, simple adaptations make significant differences, yet the interplay between housing tenure, design, and household resources leaves many vulnerable people, particularly those in private renting, students, and susceptible households (such as those with disabilities or other forms of physical frailty) as repeat victims. In short, it is hard to advance human security when households are not capable of such basic defenses.

Finally, there is the home as a site in its own right, the theater of social relations in which actors are, to a greater or lesser degree, violent, aggressive, traumatizing, and unruly toward their neighbors, their kin, or those others with whom they might share a home. The home as a place of socialization is where we begin as social entities, generating the scripts that empower us to make sense of societies outside the front door, but it is also the site for childhood traumas and injuries that dent us or make us more prone to conduct in line with prevailing social conventions. This complex interplay of factors and psychic demands is the heart of an increasing range of criminological interest (Gadd and Jefferson, 2007). Private households can generate twisted social codes, private names, and other very personal routines often evident in examples of damaged childhoods.

The private home can also be seen as a container housing subjects looking outward either onto a fear-inspiring world or one which is made to seem fearful via those sources that mediate the structure of that world to us, the portals of door, window, Internet connection, or TV. Still, the home is often neglected as a place where harm occurs because of the unease that any direct acknowledgment of such violence generates. The scale of domestic abuse; petty injuries; and banal, daily examples of gendered and intra-household aggression are critical here. In this sense, the homes we live in may be places of rage, conflict, and dispute while also being sites of sustenance, nurturing, and safety. Each of these dimensions of the home reflects appropriate examples to bring this framework to life in more detail.

The invasion of domestic space

Domestic burglary is by no means an insignificant crime, either in material or emotional terms. The FBI report that victims of burglary lost an estimated $4.6 billion in property (FBI, 2010). Reflection on this cost and material loss belies a much more important element of the occurrence of burglary—its profound and enduring emotional impact on victims, and also the fear of occurrence by those who may not have been touched by the crime. From the accounts of many international burglars in systematic research, we know that what drives this problem is a need for resources; money to pay bills or for drugs; and disregard for others, of whom the burglar often knows very little, either of their personal lives or the impact of their actions.

Although many people tend to think of the United Kingdom as a low-crime society, analysis of available international data on burglary victimization shows that the United Kingdom experiences one of the highest levels of burglary victimization of all the Western nations, albeit one that has declined markedly since the mid-1990s. The annual rate of burglary for the United Kingdom, the United States, and Australia shows rates of 73 burglaries per 10,000 people in the United States (FBI, 2010), 117 in Australia (ABS, 2013) and 121 in the United Kingdom (in 2007–8) (Home Office, 2009). The same sources find that this translated into 1.3 million domestic burglaries in the United States, 729,000 burglaries in the United Kingdom, and 259,000 in Australia.

Such data reveal little about the way that housing tenure, wealth, and neighborhood location shape the risks for households. Knowing more about these factors also contributes to a more useful, critical position that highlights how social inequalities and inequalities that are made concrete in the built environment around us influence household risks of invasion and theft. The research on burglary shows that this crime is highly susceptible to variables; in particular, home targets and the defense of the home are dramatically linked to broader social inequalities. The risks of burglary are more profoundly focused on those with few resources or incentives to defend their home using basic techniques, such as effective locks. Burglary is significant not only because of the loss of possessions but because, more often, it is the unsettling prospect of its occurrence and its psychological impact that remain the core of many people's concerns and also because these possessions reflect critical elements of our private and public identities (Goldsack, 1999).

In the United Kingdom, the United States, and Australia, the geography, tenure, and types of houses most at risk for burglary are comparable. In each case, they are homes in poor areas, flats, and rented accommodations that have the highest risk. Risk is also increased by living in a household with a single adult and children, where a head of household is young or where occupants are from a minority ethnic group (Walker et al., 2009). In Australia, rented homes have a significantly higher break-in victimization rate (4.7%) than homes that are owned (2.9%), which closely follows the British pattern (ABS, 2013).

National-level data on burglary patterns mask wide variations in the patterns of victimization between urban and rural areas, house types, and social geographies. For example, the International Crime and Victimization Survey indicates that London had a rate of 4.5% (nearly one in twenty households), which, out of seventeen national capitals, was second only to Istanbul at 4.6% of households. Stereotypes about the natural incidence of such crimes are also out of sync with reality. In particular, this reveals that the rate reported for New York was only 1.9%, close to Sydney's rate of 2.2% (Van Dijk, Van Kestern, and Smit, 2007). In the United Kingdom, London also did not have the highest statistical risk of burglary at 130 per 10,000 households; the highest was Nottingham at 180 per 10,000 (West Yorkshire and Manchester, both heavily urbanized and in generally poor areas, also feature highly).

Work regarding the activities of burglars and their targeting of particular kinds of properties bears out some of the main theoretical treatments of the increase of crime in the postwar period dealt with by routine activity theory (Cohen and Felson, 1979). This posited that much crime was predicated on the confluence of three key factors: motivated offenders, suitable targets, and absence of capable guardians. These generated or hindered the availability of targets, though said little about why offenders should be motivated to act in this way. Analysts like Tim Hope (2000) argued that a number of factors explain the postwar pattern of property crime. The increasing pattern of women at work meant that homes were left "unguarded" in ways that were previously uncommon. Thus, a major tenet of routine activity theory, the absence of a capable guardian, became an increasingly common feature of the residential landscape. Hope also argued that rising affluence and the growth of valuable and potentially mobile consumer products meant that more homes became worthwhile targets. This point has changed quite dramatically in recent years with the reduction in the relative resale value of many of these products and their increased portability. More recently, many potential burglars have turned to street robberies or other avenues that are more profitable as a result of these technological changes and the increased fortification of homes.

Overall, the BCS shows that households with no home security measures were more than ten times more likely to have been victims of burglary than those with security measures like deadlocks on doors (25.0% compared with 2.3%). According to the 2007–8 BCS, there were 502 burglaries per 10,000 households in the 20% most deprived areas, and there were 215 burglaries per 10,000 households in the 20% least deprived areas. Thus as Hope (2000) argues, the rich and poor have what he terms "different risk positions" in relation to this kind of crime, which are embedded into the broader inequalities of capitalist economies.

It is also worth bearing in mind that critical criminological viewpoints that stress declines in rates of burglary also need to acknowledge the impacts on victims and the fact that although burglary rates are now much lower than in the mid-1990s, the general rate of risk to burglary in the last thirty years is significantly higher than at any time in the twentieth century. Similarly, we need to be aware that for certain groups and locations, the risks of both victimization and repeated forms of intrusion remain very important concerns and that these are highly dependent on low levels of household resource. Further, it is critical to recognize that the bulk of fortification practices, insurance options, and other defensive practices tend to accrue to those with most resources. The predation on those with little by those with little has not seemed to reduce anxieties about home invasion among higher-income groups that remain motivated to exit social space to inhabit gated communities and fortress homes as marks of distinction and outward hostility to general social contact.

Abuse and violence inside the home

The final dimension or meaning of home we explore relates to the domestic dwelling as a site of harm. In surveys from around the world, 10–69% of women report being physically assaulted by an intimate male partner at some point in their lives. Very young children are at greatest risk: homicide rates among children aged 0–4 years are more than twice those among children aged 5–14 years (5.2 per 100,000 compared with 2.1 per 100,000). About 20% of women and 5–10% of men have suffered sexual abuse as children (WHO, 2014). In the United Kingdom, there were an estimated 12.9 million incidents of domestic *violence* in the preceding year, and more than a third (36%) of people, predominantly women, experience domestic violence during their lifetimes. Similarly, more than half (54%) of rapes in the United Kingdom are committed by a woman's current or former partner (Walby and Allen, 2004). Perhaps the most chilling figure is that two women a week, on average, are killed by a male partner or former partner; this constitutes around one-third of all female homicide victims in the United Kingdom.

These appalling data belie the simple fact that such violence and abuse takes place primarily in the domestic home, a space that is largely and sometimes wholly outside the conventional spaces of policing or community surveillance. Rykwert (1991) observed in his early work on domestic violence and abuse that these problems

> rendered problematic the notion of the home as a safe haven. Research into rape in marriage, domestic violence and sexual harassment unhinged the view that women need not fear men that they know: work colleagues, boyfriends, partners and relatives. The recognition of the familiar and the familial as no more trustworthy than the stranger put a very different complexion on who is and who is not to be trusted and, by implication, what places, times and people were risky. (p. 54)

If the home has been opened to angst over diffuse threats from outside, official data confirm that it is more often the locus of peril. Many of our most significant terrors are reserved for the mundane routines of household life: intra-familial harassment, physical and sexual abuse, and violence. It has become a social truism and statistical fact that most accidents happen in the home, but most homicides and cases of violence and abuse also occur here, not least because of the invisibility and possible prevention of detection. Domestic abuse is played out in what we habitually consider "the privacy of our own homes." This has led researchers like Elizabeth Stanko (1990) to suggest that distinctions in relation to violence can be made between the generally private, domestic clustering of primarily female victimization, and the generally more public forms of male victimization. This implies that what goes on behind closed doors is partially beyond the regulatory mechanisms of society, including surveillance, policing, and judicial and communal sanctions. When we are at home, our actions are generally invisible to such oversight and make the home feel like a space of relative emancipation, but this quality also creates a space in which the cruelest aspects of human nature can operate without prevention or hindrance.

The balance between the privacy of the home and the right of the state to intrude to prevent harm is a contentious issue, not least because freedom from any form of intrusion is seen as a cornerstone of liberal democracies. The revelation of family violence or child abuse, precisely because of a lack of such intervention, raises continued questions about approaches to "private" problems such as these. The idea that the home was a private and morally incorruptible space was deeply entrenched until the late twentieth century, when the "problem" of domestic abuse was more clearly acknowledged.

This discussion has enumerated three essential dimensions of home in relation to aspects of crime and harm, yet there are numerous other topics worthy of mention in such deliberations. It is clear that the rise of new information and communication technologies repositioned the home relative to a series of potential vulnerabilities that pass beyond or between the physical defenses of the home. For example, the use of the Internet, mobile phones, and social networking sites have largely supplanted concerns with problems like nuisance phone callers or door-to-door salespeople. New concerns are focused on problems like identity theft, whereby criminal activity is generated through the adoption of other identities to access credit or pay for goods and services. In the United Kingdom, the 2006–7 British Crime Survey reported about 48,000 account takeovers and 59,000 fraudulent applications of plastic card ID in 2006. Although recording large increases, ID theft remains only a small part of such crimes, now totaling £34 million ($52.4 million) in losses associated with this form of theft (2007). In the United States, the US Bureau of Justice Statistics for 2005 showed that 6.7% of households experienced some form of identity theft, yet only 1.1 million households discovered misuse of personal information (such as a Social Security number), just less than 1% of households.

The safety of children while using the Internet is another cause for anxiety. This highlights further areas of concern for the relative safety and security of young members of the household who may not be adequately supervised by parents, who misunderstand the nature of particular kinds of predation, or whose parents may not be sufficiently aware of these risks. For example, in the United States in 2006, 62,480,584 reports were made to the CyberTipline relating to the possession, manufacture, and distribution of child pornography, as well as 6,384 reports concerning children enticed online into sexual acts.

Exercises

1. What are some of the main problems of crime in relation to the home?
2. To what extent is gender key to understanding the question of harm and violence in relation to the home?
3. Discuss the extent to which the private life of the home can be considered in relation to a wider culture of fear.

Conclusion

What added value comes from charting the relationship between the home and questions of crime and social harm? The most pertinent response to this question is perhaps to understand how the domestic home is the site upon which some of the most globally significant forms of crime and social harm are enacted every day. Considering the need for an effective criminology of the modern, domestic home, we are necessarily reminded of the general public and political emphasis made on risks that are external to the home. This emphasis appears disproportionate and misaligned with the extent and profound damage of domestic abuse and violence. Research in this area shows familial and household environments regularly toxic in relation to their members, and this burden of victimhood primarily falls on women and children, who suffer acute psychic damage and developmental hindrance. This undermines how we should understand the family and the home: as sources of protection within our contemporary culture, places that are widely linked to notions of self-reliance, yet also a confined space in which our worst nightmares are most likely to be realized. These deep contradictions of the home are barely recognized in the habits of discourse we find surrounding domestic life precisely because the reality of such horrors is more easily repressed than acknowledged.

Although most of us feel safe at home, the place of the private realm is frequently revealed to us through news and film media as a façade behind which regular forms of abuse and violence are enacted. At the same time, as the home is the stage upon which such harms take place, it is a critical point of mediation by which we learn about and prepare for the risks associated with the world outside, hearing of such danger through news and other information conduits received in the home.

Technological change has also opened the way for new forms of potential harm, some of which are sexually predatory in nature. The fears we have when we are in our homes might be based on prior experiences or may be "imported" into our consciousness through contact with crime dramas and alarming news items in newspapers and the Internet. Although we may feel that the source of possible attack might come in the form of burglary or unwanted visitors, the kind of physical defenses put in place to allay our fear of these occurrences—alarms, locks and fisheye viewers—do little to assuage the anxieties generated by news media and information flows permitted entry to our home-world via television, computer, and mobile phone screens.

If the home is our castle, then pursuing this metaphor further, the social relationships within it can be opened up as so many mini-fiefdoms in which sexual power and the extraction of duty and allegiance are played out each day. We live in societies in which the meaning of home is laden with the suggestion of civility, civilization, independence, escape, and freedom, when it is as much the case that our homes may become at times the very reverse of these qualities.

7 Home Economics

Introduction

What do sociologists have to offer on the analysis of the economy and its connections to the domestic home? We have already suggested that the private home is part of a much larger range of social and economic factors and that much of this is mediated through public politics. What happens to owners, renters, the embedded nature of housing, and its construction and sale in the wider economy are critical to the enactment of politics. In this chapter, we consider these issues and the important links between housing as a financial asset and the "financialization" (the creation of new and complex products and financial instruments to enable new markets and the creation of value) in Western economies. The current global financial crisis was generated in large part by the antics of politicians, banks, and the drivers of capitalism as a system as these efforts became focused on housing. More than ever, housing is implicated in the direct workings of an increasingly complex and global economic system predicated on the number and value of house purchases and sales (Sassen, 2012), bearing important consequences for cities, localities, and individual households (Fields, 2013), whether or not they own their own homes.

The financial crisis has revealed how critical housing—its purchase, sale, and the financial instruments that facilitate these transactions—is to the economies of the Western world. As we argue, this is not so much because housing is important in generating the jobs of builders, joiners, and craftspeople, though this remains significant as an economic concern, but rather because the trade in homes and newfound trade in the debt supporting that trade came to unravel the booming economies of the United Kingdom and the United States and countries like Ireland, Greece, and Spain. In short, to understand fully the means by which housing systems are produced and consumed, we must look at the contemporary political and economic situation to reveal the inner workings of contemporary societies that have placed so much emphasis on the role of home ownership as an indicator of economic vitality. The risks of such a view and its wider social impacts are vital issues that are explored in this chapter.

Home ownership has become a vehicle by which consumer spending is expanded by offering credit through home loans backed by mortgages, often to less well-off households. This has had the effect of generating major risks because these households were more likely to default on their repayments. The response of banks was to uncouple the risks generated by this lending by selling these mortgage-backed debts because many such loans were made to households employed precariously or simply subsisting on low incomes and might not be able to pay such debts. Considering the details of the recent history of social and economic change, the important point to remember is that this is only the most recent crisis in capitalism linked to housing fortunes (e.g., successive downturns have affected house prices, construction by private suppliers, and supply in the 1920s, 1940s, 1970s, and 1990s, across much of the Western world) and comes merely as the most recent example of problems generated by the necessity for capitalism to grow, in this case through modifications around the financial products available to prospective home buyers (Langley, 2008). Here we consider the roots of the current crisis as a case study of the socioeconomic processes involved around the provision of housing, but we also consider the analytical tools and insights developed by sociologists who have sought to understand the workings of housing finance and political life (Bourdieu, 2005). We also consider the importance of housing markets and owner occupation to the wider social 'feel-good' factors underlying electoral success (the application of low interest rates in countries like the United States, United Kingdom, and Australia, and the British example of the "right to buy" public housing assets by tenants, e.g.). In this complex context, the role of sociologists in unpacking how markets (macro and micro) operate through social practices, their political imperatives, and systemic drivers (described by analysts like Marx and recently by David Harvey) is essential to more effective sociological understandings of how the social and economic worlds around us operate.

Capital, financialization, and the circuits of capital accumulation

One of the most insightful ways to understand how housing markets operate is provided by the Marxist geographer David Harvey. As we stated earlier, Harvey rejects the notion that government interventions in the housing market are simply there for the common good. Instead, he argues that government policies are primarily geared to generating economic growth and profits for property developers, mortgage lenders, house buyers, and rental investors seeking to maximize their profits (Harvey, 2010). Harvey's work importantly exposes the roots of the financial crisis as being traced to inadequate housing policy. We now comprehend what, at the time, notably had not been second-guessed by almost any economists or economic sociologists: some of the factors leading to the global financial crisis in 2008 stemmed from the failure of successive governments to build sufficient public housing that met the needs of low-income US households and from the ways many people, even those on very low incomes, sought to enter home ownership with the lure of making small (and indeed sometimes very large) personal fortunes. With no alternative available, low-income households were encouraged to incur large debts purchasing homes (see Aalbers, 2012, for a discussion). As elsewhere, home ownership in the United States has been marketed as a means to wealth, to achieve one's dreams, and to live a happy life. The high costs of the private rental market and lack of public housing made the allure of home ownership even more compelling; this mix of economic, social, and political factors generates a complex range of forces that must be understood and which illuminate a much wider set of processes affecting the position of housing in society and its sustainability for those in it. As we will see, many people literally lost their homes as a result of the ensuing crisis, while banks and other institutions were bailed out and protected by governments that could not allow such fundamental actors in capitalist economies to fail with the spotlight on them. Although the gains of processes of financialization accrued to many in the banking sector, the major losers were precariously employed households that could not maintain the increasingly costly mortgage products once the initial low-rate periods ended. As writers like Sassen (2012) have convincingly argued, the sociological implications of this are now all too evident, with predatory capitalist institutions and actors snapping up the resulting super-cheap assets only to subsequently rent back to these very same low-income households in many cases (Fields, 2013).

The ideology of home ownership is so entrenched in countries such as the United States, Australia, New Zealand, and the United Kingdom, that our conception of self and its actualization is often understood to be deeply bound up with owning a home (Allon and Redden, 2012). We feel diminished (what Bauman [2004: 39] has termed "flawed consumers") if unable to own a home, so it is no wonder that people take huge risks to secure mortgages. For a complex set of reasons, governments have also promoted the ideology of home ownership. First, there are huge profits to be made from the marketing and sale of homes, and governments are highly predisposed to supporting the businesses profiting from them. Secondly, governments view home ownership as a bulwark for existing social order, assuming that homeowners have vested interests in maintaining the economic order and their employment. Third, home ownership appeals to many voters because it creates a sense of security and offers the potential for generating wealth (Colic-Peisker and Johnson, 2012). Homeowners who see the value of their houses rise may be less likely to be critical of government policy making. As Harvey (2010) noted, some governments have been active in encouraging home ownership through policy reform and via the construction of an ideological narrative encouraging individuals to see themselves as responsible for their own welfare (Dupuis and Thorns, 2002). The subsidies now available in the United Kingdom for private health care, charitable "free schools," home ownership, and pensions were put in place to position "private" as the optimum choice for consumers, while funding for collectively provided services and insurances such as state pensions has been dramatically cut (Standing, 2011). Sociologists such as Ulrich Beck (2009) have viewed this trend through the prism of risk in which individuals take on personal responsibility for what were once considered collective issues. Accompanying the shift toward the private over and above the collective has been a government-led narrative seeking to portray issues such as poor housing, unemployment, and bad health as personal failings rather than linking them to the effects of structural inequality. The idealization of the "private" over and above the "collective" is purposeful and has both normalized and intensified the desire for home ownership. In the United States, the United Kingdom, and Australia, right-of-center discourses have often framed government housing authorities as inept bureaucracies, unable to meet the needs of households with low incomes (Schwartz, 2010; Dorling, 2014; Jacobs, Berry, and Dalton, 2013).

The major postwar paradigm shift in government policy making has been analyzed by Forrest and Hirayama (2014). Although housing has always been a site for profit, they argue that the increasing commodification of housing has changed the way that homes are perceived and consumed by households. This change in how housing is used is different from earlier periods, when housing was usually perceived as a utility good. They predict that this intensification of the commodification of housing will lead to a proliferation of "financialized private landlordism." These efforts are increasingly internationalized and now affect the private rental market as investors seek to acquire the defunded assets now being sold by local authorities. Forrest and Hirayama show that investment companies operate as transnational landlords, buying up properties to make speculative profits. Often these investment companies offer their clients new financial instruments such as rent-backed securities. As we discuss later, Allon (2012) has also viewed this financialization of the home as a more concerted attempt at asset accumulation by homeowners, supported by governments eager to court their desires. As she writes:

> The ownership of the home is conceived as providing a direct experience of enterprise, a way of encouraging the development of long term processes of self-investment, and, importantly, an investment strategy for leveraging wealth. In the new flexible spaces of society and labour markets, individuals must now take control of their own economic lives and equip themselves with the entrepreneurial capacities necessary to recognise the intensified individual competition and market pressures of a new and deregulated economy. (Allon, 2012: 405)

For Smith and Searle (2008), Allon (2012), and Forrest and Hirayama (2014), the home has been effectively reconfigured as both an object (its adaptation, upgrading, and decoration) and as part of a strategy for realizing new rounds of speculative investment. In the United Kingdom, we can see "shared ownership" and "help to buy" schemes put in place by the government to encourage investment in the housing market as exactly the kinds of supporting policies put in place by governments viewing homeowners and home investors as a majority that need to be supported and respected (as well as owners who also rent to others and have expanded in number dramatically in recent years). One way of seeing the scale of this support is to examine the value of outstanding "buy-to-let" mortgages, used to encourage private landlordism. Lending for buy-to-let rose from £2 billion (US$3 billion) in 1998 to over £47 billion (US$72.5 billion) by 2004 (Allon, 2012: 407). In April 2013, The Bank of England provided £80bn for lenders to boost loan activity. The scheme works by offering cheap Bank of England loans to banks and building societies that lend to rental investors and small and medium business enterprises.

Politicians and the media generally view rising house prices as a proxy for a successful economy. There has been a push to encourage as many people as possible to buy homes and to encourage speculative investment in housing. In a more socially and economically just society with starkly reduced inequalities, ownership would offer a range of benefits, such as escaping a poor quality and lightly regulated rental sector (O'Sullivan and Gibb, 2012) and helping reduce housing costs in later life. Yet in a society that forms social values around home as a place of exchange value and where public housing has been reduced in quantity and quality, the inequalities increasingly pervasive in society today mean that ownership is desired as much for the possibility of making money and warding off anxieties about future income and security. The impetus for home ownership has been furthered in recent years as governments seek to unload their social responsibilities in these fields. Homeowners in the United Kingdom comprise around two-thirds of all households (though, critically, this has fallen from nearly 70% a few years ago as more rental investors, most of them themselves wealthy homeowners, outbid aspiring homeowners seeking to buy their first homes). The appeal of home ownership has been maintained further by underfunding the public housing sector and through a reluctance to regulate the private rental market. If nothing else, the result has been a reduced housing supply, stressed households making payments to keep their home and a stigmatized social rented sector. Government policies benefit an increasingly wealthy and broadly secure constituency of homeowners at the expense of renters (Malpass, 2008).

Although home ownership is still viewed as "an article of faith" by all major political parties, it is evident that political commentators and public opinion have begun to consider the negative effects the privileging of homeowners and landlords has set in motion (see Dorling, 2014). Much of the impetus for this criticism can be traced to the expense of buying property in countries like the United States and the United Kingdom. The options for young people are limited, and many have no choice but to live with their parents or buy property a long way from employment, further adding to the cost and stresses of everyday life. In London, the high cost of housing has even more pronounced effects, leading to large swaths of the city becoming zones of residential social exclusion (e.g., Kensington, St. Johns Wood, Notting Hill). Up until the 1970s, the main option for affordable housing for people with incomes was public housing, but most of the stock in these areas is no longer available, bought and sold under "right-to-buy" schemes. London as a city is becoming geographically polarized in ways that would not have been foreseen, by most people, thirty years ago. A similar story applies to other major cities such as Sydney, New York, and San Francisco; these trends already have major consequences in terms of social composition and economic impacts for these cities and their residents.

The impact inequality has on the housing market is evident when considering the private rental market in London and other major cities. The increase in rents in the private rental market has forced many young people to share accommodations, and overcrowding is increasingly common. The situation for many low-income households has been exacerbated by government legislation that caps the rent subsidies available to those tenants receiving housing benefits. The government intends to force claimants to leave their property and seek cheaper accommodations elsewhere in order reduce welfare expenditure. Such pernicious policies illuminate the logic of neoliberal governance and its social impacts; people who are often already highly vulnerable are un-housed and forced to compete in a housing market that is already overloaded; often they must leave the city entirely.

This quote from the prologue to John Lanchester's novel *Capital* helps us to understand how social change and economics have combined through the housing system and the market in homes. We can connect the mentality indicated here to the development of so-called "property porn" and the ways in which housing as a means to make money rather than as a place to live have come to dominate social thinking, as Allon and other sociologists have suggested.

People began to do up the houses, not in the ad hoc way of previous decades but with systematic make-overs in the knocking-through, open-plan style that became fashionable in the seventies and never really went away. . . . Now, however, the houses had become so valuable to people who already lived in them, and so expensive for people who had recently moved into them, that they had become central actors in their own right. This happened at first slowly, gradually, as average prices crept up through the lower hundred thousands, and then, as people from the financial industry discovered the area, and house prices in general began to rise sharply, and people began to be paid huge bonuses, bonuses that were three or four times their notional annual pay, bonuses which were big multiples of the national average salary, and a general climate of hysteria affected everything to do with house prices—then, suddenly, prices began to go up so quickly that it was as if they had a will of their own. There was a sentence that rang down the decades, a very English sentence: "Did you hear what they got for the house down the road?" (Lanchester, 2012: 3–4.)

As stated in the introduction to this chapter, one of the most insightful explanations of the housing market was proffered by David Harvey (2008, 2010). Harvey argues that the production and consumption of housing is a major generator of profits for investors and allied businesses. Housing is promoted as a commodity to be bought and sold in the market. Private property has been a vehicle to make profit, and it is for this reason much of the excess profits circulating in the global economy end up as investment in property. Nevertheless, ideologues promote the virtues of capitalism and persuade us that the desire to own a home is innate and natural (see Chapter 1). For Harvey, the reality is more prosaic; governments promote the property market as an investment opportunity for capital accumulation. The profits to be made from home ownership can only be actualized if the demand remains. Hence, the considerable effort expended by the mortgage industry, government, estate agencies, and property related businesses to promote home ownership as a vehicle to make money and succeed in the world. As he writes, "Capitalism is a class form of society given over to the perpetual production of surpluses. This means that it is always producing the necessary conditions for urbanization to occur" (Harvey, 2010: 166).

The explanation provided by Harvey helps us comprehend contemporary shifts taking place across the urban form. Consider how the geography of suburban life is changing since many purchasers buy and sell property primarily for financial gain rather than a home to reside. Suburbs can no longer be assumed as being synonymous with stability or neighborliness, where it could be presumed that neighbors are familiar with each other. The "ghost" suburban housing estates in Ireland represent an extreme failure of capitalist housing markets. Built on speculative capital, these new developments remain largely unoccupied following the collapse in housing prices in the aftermath of the GFC (Global Financial Crisis). In 2010, there were as many as 350,000 estimated vacant properties and 2,846 'ghost' estates.

Another important contribution to understanding the housing system is provided by Jamie Peck's wide-ranging analysis of neoliberalism (Peck, 2010). Peck uses the term *neoliberal* to denote the way that governments pursue a pro-business agenda and the freeing of markets as the primary means of resource allocations in an ever-expanding range of areas. He points out that the commercialization of the welfare state and housing has extended the capacity of private sector agencies to generate wealth. Peck's analysis brings to the fore how governments use ideology to justify specific interventions. He argues the importance of "approaching neoliberalism not as some automatic system, but an earthly process, realized through political action and institutional reinvention" (Peck, 2010: 33). As Peck elucidates, neoliberalism is not some free-floating abstraction that operates independently of human agency. On the contrary, it is best understood as a specific set of practices to reconfigure the agencies of government and create the conditions for private sector profitability.

Both Harvey and Peck's work help us understand actions that might appear as contradictory in the way that policy makers implement housing policy. In practice, housing policies are bifurcated in that in most instances the primary aim of government is to maintain investment opportunities for wealth accumulation, and the secondary aim is to address the problems that arise from this commitment, such as increased inequality and homelessness. As Kleinman (1998: 250) argues, in most nation-states, housing policy "is now founded in practice on the acceptance at a more or less permanent level, of a continuing divide between the haves and have-nots in each country. In housing policy, this underlying belief finds expression in the retreat of national governments from responsibility for achieving more equal outcomes." In this context, the idea that "public" housing should be a low-cost and high-quality alternative is no longer taken seriously by many politicians, ensuring that the accommodation needs of many low-income households remain unmet.

Harvey (2008, 2010, and 2014) considers 'crisis' as an endemic feature of contemporary capitalism. His view of the 2008 global financial crisis portrays nothing unique in the way it unfolded; the recurrence of housing bubbles and mortgage default can be viewed as inevitable outcomes. He adopts a historical overview to show the continuity of crisis afflicting capitalism, using examples in 1850s France, 1930s United States, and 1970s Europe. He argues that the recession of the 1930s in the United States was resolved through a program of suburbanization, which was a means for the government to overcome the contradictions within the capitalist system. In an article published in 1998, he summarized his understanding of suburbanization:

> The suburbanization of the United States was not merely a matter of new infrastructures. As in Second Empire Paris, it entailed a radical transformation in lifestyles, bringing new products from housing to refrigerators and air conditioners, as well as two cars in the driveway and an enormous increase in the consumption of oil. It also altered the political landscape, as subsidized home-ownership for the middle classes changed the focus of community action towards the defence

> of property values and individualized identities, turning the subur-
> ban vote towards conservative republicanism. (Harvey, 2008: 27)

The present housing crisis can be traced to the suppression of wage demands in the late 1980s and 1990s. Although this may have reduced upward pressure on inflation, it also reduced overall demand for goods and services and hence, profitability. The way out of this impasse, according to Harvey, was to encourage wage earners to supplement their income with private credit. The ease of mortgages and growth in credit card lending was the main reason why countries such as the United Kingdom and the United States were able to sustain economic growth in the 1980s and 1990s. The risk of private indebtedness and housing bubbles was overlooked.

The high level of debt both public and private remains a serious threat for the economies, but the current government in the United Kingdom sought to boost demand by a combination of printing more money (quantitative easing) and stimulating the owner-occupied hous-ing market, offering security for mortgages taken out by first-time homeowners—further lures by governments to help placate prospective owners and to act as implicit subsidies to the house development sector. The expectation is that this will increase demand and lead to spending in housing-related areas of the economy such as home furnishing, house maintenance, and so on. The UK government has also been quite happy to tolerate significant house price inflation in London (25% in 2013–14), fueled by speculative investment from foreign investors. Concisely, large increases of foreign investment in the London property market help reduce the balance of payment deficit. This deficit is one of the factors that determine the interest rates banks charge on government debt.

Harvey is pessimistic with regard to the capability of governments to resolve the current crisis. In contrast to the 1930s and 1940s, there is not the scope to enact measures that enable consumers to incur large-scale debts. In the 1990s, this was possible by encouraging consumers to take out subprime mortgages. The large debts incurred and risk of default were not considered a problem by policy makers or a risk to banks once subprime mortgages were bundled and traded as commodi-ties. In 2001, nearly 40% of the total proportion of all US debt (gov-ernment and private) was mortgage-market related. As John Lanchester (2010) notes, in 2007, it was possible for low-income borrowers to gain approval for 100% mortgages without showing employment earnings or providing substantive evidence of collateral. The impetus for sub-prime mortgages was sustained by the finance service industry lobbying activities (Gotham, 2011). In 2001, subprime mortgages accounted for 7% of the total mortgage market in the United States (Courchrane and Kogut, 2012). Harvey (2010) explains how the risk of indebtedness was overcome. He writes that

> all this indebtedness was obviously risky, but that could be taken care of by the wondrous financial innovations of securitisation that supposedly spread the risk around and even created the illusion that risk had disappeared. Fictitious financial capital took control and nobody wanted to stop it because everyone who mattered seemed to be making lots of money. (p. 17)

As pointed out earlier, large amounts of surplus capital currently in circulation are now being invested in what are seen as viable safe property havens, global cities such as Shanghai, Sydney, London, Vancouver, Hong Kong, and New York, and it is one of the primary reasons for the increase in property prices in recent years. We can see this clearly in the London market, where as much as 40% of all property investment is from overseas (this figure is much higher for both new build and inner London "super prime" areas). House prices and rents across the capital have increased, with all the negative social consequences that ensue for those on low incomes and those without capital, while those with the resources made vast amounts of additional wealth.

Harvey argues that at some point in the future, a similar crisis will occur, as over investment will lead to a property bubble and eventual crash. He views urbanization as only a short-term fix, although its pattern of development defines the form of the next crisis. Sustained investments in the built environment, he argues, "are typically credit-based, high-risk and long in the making: when over investment is finally revealed (as happened in Dubai) then the financial mess that takes many years to produce takes many years to unwind" (Harvey, 2010: 10). In the past, governments committed funds for urbanization as a response to the crisis, and the form it takes can reveal what the next crisis will look like. In the 1940s, the US federal government put in place subsidies that ensconced the automobile culture and a way of life that has proved both self-perpetuating and hard to change (suburban development and its reliance on plentiful and cheap oil has raised grave concerns about sustainability). This is one of the reasons why policies to address climate change have proved so difficult. Householders find it difficult to change their lifestyles, and they want to maintain their standards of living.

The financialization of "everyday life"

In the first part of this chapter, we stated that the commodification of housing has been driven by commercial interests in spite of the obvious long-term negative implications. One of Marx's most important insights was to identify the generative component of capitalism, that is, enterprises strive by seeking new opportunities for profit and creating demands for products by manufacturing an emptiness, a sense of need and desire in consumers. Over the course of the last thirty years there have been orchestrated attempts by financial services industries to encourage homeowners to draw equity from their homes for spending. As Susan Smith shows (Smith, 2007; Smith, Searle, and Cook, 2008; Smith and Searle, 2008), housing is far more than a place of shelter; it has now become an investment good that homeowners use to generate wealth. The fascinating aspect of the financialization of "everyday life" is the manner in which ideology has been internalized as somehow "natural" and of our own volition. We think the desire to make money from our home is viewed as common sense; the problematic and societal implications of this logic are suppressed. It can be argued that the ideology of advanced capitalism requires a form of cognitive dissonance. For us to participate in the variegated forms of capitalism requires us to suppress or downplay our wider anxieties in relation to sociality and collective belonging (Zizek, 1989, 2011).

The financialization of everyday life, and in particular the home, helps us understand the increased interest in home "makeovers" and TV programs focused on buying and selling property. The Australian academic Fiona Allon's (2008) book *Renovation Nation* portrayed the appeal of the home as now bound together with its financial capability to generate income and social status. She argues that we take care of the home because it offers up opportunities to maintain social status and wealth. We already mentioned the work of Susan Smith and Beverley Searle (2008), who explain new financial products that are being devised so homeowners can use their property as a security for old age or as a vehicle to transfer funds to their offspring or close relatives. In short, the transformation of housing from a consumption good in which people derive satisfaction from living and obtaining shelter to one in which it can also deliver a profit (an investment good) is underway. As Allon (2012: 406) writes, "The home, in turn, functions less as a space of shelter and refuge and more as a site of financial calculation, able to be viewed dispassionately as one of the many other potential savings and investment vehicles."

Although all these financial products may appear attractive, there are important societal implications. First, the opportunities afforded to homeowners for wealth creation are not available to renters (both public and private) so that the use of these products is likely to extend social inequalities related to wealth. Second, the financialization of the home leads householders to extend their debts to pay for goods. Although this model might appear viable when house prices are rising, there are associated risks: for example, high interest rates, unemployment or a fall in house prices could lead to householders extending their debt and risking their homes. Third, the pursuit of profit changes our societal relations with each other and our sense of self. It encourages us to view our relations with others as instrumental rather than as intrinsically worthwhile.

Saskia Sassen (2012: 221) provides an incisive commentary on the risks that are associated with housing debt. In the United States, as many as 13 million households had no option other than to foreclose their mortgage because of a sharp fall in housing prices and rising unemployment. She writes that the current era is "a space of expulsion, in contrast to the Keynesian epoch where the systematic edge was a space of incorporation, not because it was an ideal period but because the constitutive systematicities were about mass production and mass consumption." Sassen makes connections between different forms of exploitation and exclusion that cut across national boundaries. The predatory lending practices that led to the GFC are constitutive of an established form of capitalist exploitation that has thus far met with little resistance from governments that see their primary role as propping up or creating new spaces and opportunities for profit.

Exercises

1. Consider what the social value of a home is (its use value), and discuss these in relation to the idea of exchange value (the value of a home in terms of its sale and exchange).
2. Is it possible that governments might begin to view collective forms of housing provision as a desirable way to address housing need?
3. How closely is government linked to the aspirations of banks and other financial institutions seeking to make money from the production and consumption of homes?
4. To what extent does home ownership act as a form of social division today?

Conclusion

In this chapter, we considered how the home has become an instrument for profit. We can trace this change to new formations of capitalist development that now extend beyond the world of work and also to areas of home life and leisure in ways that would have been difficult to predict just forty years ago. The commodification of the home is now so entrenched that we view it as normal and natural. Yet, as Sassen and Allon report, its commodification is symptomatic of wider economic formations. Here, too, the work of David Harvey is prescient; the surplus profits made from extracting value from labor are in circulation, looking for opportunities to generate investment returns. The property market and its allied industries are seen as a stable and relatively risk free opportunity to extend wealth assets. As Allon (2008: 208) writes, "Home ownership became convenient and persuasive shorthand for a set of ideas that received substantial political encouragement and support: financial initiative and aspiration, individual success and achievement, and traditional families and communities."

There is a social risk to this financialization of everyday life, as writers such as Bauman (2000) and Lash (1999) point out. We imbue much of our identity in our home to the extent that many traditional social relationships, acquired through friendships and work colleagues, are often deemed of secondary importance. Our personalities are now equated more than before with our wealth, and this also explains our interest in the very rich and celebrity culture. In short, the ideology of neoliberalism has furnished a societal culture that valorized material wealth over and above other forms of living. Harvey describes (2012: 14) the modern era in the following way: "This is a world in which the neoliberal ethic of intense possessive individualism can become the template for human personality socialization. The impact is increasing individualistic isolation, anxiety and neurosis."

Finally, we can see already some reaction to what happened. The "occupy movements" that congregated in cities across the globe, is one obvious example, but we can also detect a more critical engagement with the ideologies of capitalism and an awareness of its effects on our modes of relations with each other. Politics is difficult to predict, but as ever-increasing numbers of young people are unable to purchase their homes and have to rely on the private rental market for housing, we will see pressure to reform applied to the housing market, driving it to spread wealth more equitably and to place curbs on the opportunities that are now available for homeowners and rental investors making significant profits purely on the basis of property ownership. In other words, housing is likely to resurface as a source of tension and fissure in contemporary society.

8 Housing, State and Market

Introduction

We have considered the argument that home ownership is in some way natural or desirable: discussions of the different forms of occupation in any dwelling tend to come back to distinctions between renting from a private landlord, purchase, or renting from the state or state-subsidized landlords such as housing associations. Our focus in this chapter is why and how Western nation-states feel obliged to offer housing assistance by building and renting homes, primarily to low income and poor households. What is the state's role in these processes, and why is this important form of provision increasingly neglected in recent decades? Drawing on social histories of housing and critical theories of the role of the state, we will examine the arguments that are used to advance public house building programs and consider how important public forms of housing provision have been in lifting the living conditions of poorer households, serving broader aims for work- and war-ready workers, reducing the need for rising pay by workers, and quelling social unrest and revolution more broadly. Public housing continues to provoke deep questions about the role of the welfare state.

For some commentators, public housing is the "wobbly pillar" of the welfare state because it has been portrayed by its critics as a reinforcing dependency (Torgersen, 1987; Malpass, 2005), and access to public housing remains a problem for constituencies on the political right (witness the recent discussion of a removal of lifetime rights to public housing in the United Kingdom). For both benevolent campaigners and actors working to reduce the costs of welfare, public housing has become a point of contention in many Western countries. The critical result of this has been a significant reduction and diversification of public housing programs. There are recently many more providers (such as state-regulated housing associations and cooperatives) and a broader decline in funding and entitlements to public housing, which signals the public perception of public housing as deeply problematic and fundamentally linked to its role as a residual provider of housing of last resort to the "mad, the bad, and the sad." Attacks on the state's rationale for such provision have also led to policies like the "right to buy," which have further weakened the state's ability to provide housing for those in need. In short, issues of inequality, access, and the needs of capital for labor remain at the forefront of debates about the tenurial systems and conditions of housing in even the most "advanced" Western economies.

The myth of the benevolent state

Often, it is assumed that the state acts benevolently to meet the housing needs of low-income households through interventions in the housing market such as social housing funding and housing benefits in the private rental sector. One reason such an assumption holds sway is that governments and policy makers spend considerable resources to convince us this is the case. Press releases, policy documents, ministerial announcements, and media briefings on housing are all intended to portray the government as acting to mitigate problems in the housing market. In this chapter, we argue that such a view of housing policy is flawed. Instead, to understand the role of the state in matters of housing, we must recognize that the state primarily serves the interests of homeowners and rental investors over and above disadvantaged social groups (Lowe, 2011).

As we argue, the primary aim of many governments is to deliver economic growth, pursued through processes of neoliberalization. The current UK austerity program to reduce welfare expenditures (such as housing benefits and public housing) is justified on claims it encourages competiveness, deters welfare dependency, and reduces the need to raise tax. In countries such as the United States, United Kingdom, and Australia, public housing is not considered a priority compared to welfare expenditures on health and education. In part, the low priority accorded to public housing reflects the inability of housing lobbyists to persuade the government to invest more, and the capacity of the house building and financial lobbyists to convince government to subsidize homeowners and to offer financial incentives for private rental investors and first-time home buyers. Historically, UK housing policy has favored the affluent over and above the socially disadvantaged in successive governments (see Harloe, 1995). Rather than the state operating benevolently in housing-related matters, on many occasions its policies serve to enhance the opportunities for wealth creation among the already better-off and thereby accentuate social inequality. This argument will be unpopular with policy makers and professionals working for government organizations, who claim, with some justification, that they seek to improve the conditions of the homeless through a plethora of initiatives and programs. Our point is that these initiatives, though worthy, are of little help in mitigating the effects stemming from the pursuit of neoliberal economic objectives.

There are, of course, external factors that have an impact on policy making. In the United Kingdom and similar nation-states, immigration and declining mortality rates have led to an increase in population. For example, in the United States, Chicago, Dallas-Fort Worth, and Houston are projected to become megacities, like New York and Los Angeles, as the metropolitan area population rises above 10 million by 2040. In the United Kingdom, London and the South East of England is the largest rising region; over the next ten years, the capital's population will grow by an anticipated 100,000 persons per year, according to government estimates. As discussed in earlier chapters, there has also been an increase in single occupancy households due to people living longer, higher rates of family breakup, and a decline in cohabitation. In addition, more young people are living with parents because of the high rental and home prices. These changes create profound stresses on the housing system, while suggesting the ongoing need for central coordination and planning by governments to predict and counteract the resulting social tensions and distress that such conditions generate.

In the United Kingdom, we can see a decline in real incomes over the years, particularly among workers in traditionally low-income jobs. The government's capacity to rein in wage demands and keep a lid on inflation has been one of the factors leading to more dual-income households as they seek to keep up with the cost of housing in particular. The shortfall in the amount of housing needed (currently only about 120,000 homes are being built each year), is now as low as it was in the 1920s (see Figure 8.1). In both the United Kingdom and the United States, house building has declined significantly. This can be highlighted by gathering the data on the number of private homes completed each year (this does not include housing built by the state) and giving these figures as a rate per million population so that the two countries' levels of building activity can be compared. These figures highlight the much higher historical delivery of private units in the United States, but a decline to the trend level found in the United Kingdom. The shortfall in low-cost housing has led to longer waiting lists for social housing and to overcrowding and growing homelessness.

Figure 8.1 Number of private homes completed each year, United States and United Kingdom, 1970–2013, per million population.

Source: US Census Bureau; UK Dept of Communities and Local Government.

Proponents of neoliberal ideas have successfully framed a version of politics that makes it difficult to propose alternative models of resource allocation, while attenuating the role of the state as an effective provider. All of the major political parties share similar policies, including the deployment of market mechanisms within the public sector, low taxation rates, and budget setting to ensure welfare expenditure remains tightly controlled. Although differences in approach exist, both UK Labour and Conservative and Liberal Democrat parties in government have prioritized the maintenance of house prices and private-sector profitability as their main objectives.

In the specific example of public housing, successive UK governments enacted a series of measures to marginalize the sector. For example, the 1980 Housing Act provided subsidies for tenants to buy their property at lower than market rates, a policy that reduced the proportion of public housing to let. In addition, the Conservative government led by Margaret Thatcher imposed rules that prevented local authorities from using more than 25% of their capital receipts on renewing their stock. The shortfall in funds for public housing was briefly addressed by the Labour government in the 1990s when as much as £19 billion (US$29.3 billion) was set aside for social housing investment. Overall, the shortage of public housing and the high demand has led to local authorities tightening allocation protocols, which further residualized the sector. As local authorities are denied resources to maintain public housing, the government has increased the subsidies for private-sector landlords investing in property. Much of the profit that landlords make is a consequence of public housing marginalization and the switch of subsidies in the form of housing benefit.

Understanding the state's role in relation to housing

As indicated in the introduction, the dominant framework for understanding housing policy positions the state as largely benevolent in its intentions, seeking to address social problems as they arise. As we argue, such a perspective is both conceptually flawed and simplistic. There are more critical and effective ways of understanding the state's role in housing. Some of the most insightful are the Marxist interpretations enunciated by authors such as Ball (1983); Ball, Harloe, and Martens (1988); and Harloe (1995). All of these authors argue that government interventions are undertaken to maximize opportunities for profit. In particular, Ball has been critical of housing policy perspectives that place too much emphasis on consumption practices. In his view, the profits from production operate as the main concern of government. In his book *Housing Policy and Economic Power* (1983), he writes:

> In terms of the economy as a whole, the interests of capital frequently appear as inevitable, quasi-natural economic necessities. Economic growth, for example, is equated with capital accumulation; new investment generally is posed as the problem of encouraging new private investment (via inducements, not directives); improvements in labour productivity have to be on capital's terms, for instance. (Ball 1983: 361)

He continues to argue that there is considerable pressure on any government to establish policies that reduce living standards at a time of economic crisis. Harloe pursues a similar line of argument; he writes:

> The private market provision for the mass of the population as a capitalist commodity, and the system of private property ownership on

which this provision rests, has been a core element in the capitalist organisation of society and the economy from the earliest years. Historically, industrial, property and the financial capital has been the motive force driving the system. (1995: 3)

Harloe notes that major interventions to support social housing took place after both world wars when the market was unable to address the requirements of industry for profitability. Rather than see government intervention as a response to pressing *social* need, it was economic necessity behind the low-cost housing. To such structural interpretations we can add other factors that help to explain the increasing preparedness of governments to intervene, including rent strikes, the popularity of supporting the needs of soldiers returning from the Second World War, and other political action by groups and parties determined to affect the level and quality of housing provision.

Both Ball and Harloe stress the importance of housing in terms of production. A different vantage point but an equally critical perspective was advanced by Jim Kemeny (1992). Drawing upon the insights of Weberian theory, Kemeny (1992) emphasizes the housing policy context as one where competing interest groups vie for influence. These include consumers (primarily homeowners), producers (the housing industry), and welfare agencies and their representatives (groups such as Shelter and Crisis). Policy decisions are often shaped by lobbyists and pressure groups to influence government. We can identify the key groupings as homeowners, banks and mortgage lenders, volume house builders, and estate agencies. These tensions create a contested landscape in which the various important actors and institutions seek to frame public debate and the main issues at hand. Despite this, it has been the visions of government in consort with developers and housing financiers that won as a result of their social power and ability to frame their views most effectively.

In the next section of this chapter, we show how commitment to public housing has waxed and waned in the postwar period, noting the capacity of interest groups to influence policy. Two important periods can be identified. The first encompasses the years from 1945 to the mid-1970s. This was a period in which successive governments were willing to invest in public housing, though the Conservative Party was more focused on promoting owner occupation (Malpass and Murie, 1987). The second period is the mid-1970s, when UK government was forced to borrow money from the International Monetary Fund to meet debt obligations in that previous era of austerity. Over the last forty years, attitudes within many national governments (particularly in Treasury departments) have hardened to the extent that public housing is now seen as a drain on resources and a tenure that entrenches welfare dependency. The attack on public housing has been largely successful; it has very little support within government or among the public at large. Later on, we suggest the attack on public housing serves a wider ideological purpose, namely, to enhance the appeal of home ownership and provide a rationale for the marketization of local authority housing departments.

To understand the reasons why governments committed funds for public housing from the mid-1930s, we must appreciate the rapid industrialization of the United Kingdom in the nineteenth century. The population of Britain's cities, such as London, Glasgow, Birmingham, and Manchester, increased exponentially as households moved from rural locations to find work. The housing conditions for the poorest residents were abject, and both overcrowding and ill health were common features. Although social reformers advocated public health reforms, there was no collective organization advocating for public housing. The significant change in attitudes can be sourced to the end of the Great War, when the emergence of the UK Labour party, both at a municipal and national level, made the case for house building programs to improve conditions. The 1919 UK Town and Country Planning Act established protocols for large house building programs, but it was not until the late 1920s and 1930s that these programs were progressed through slum clearance and new housing projects initiated by municipal Labour authorities.

Although these building projects were significant and enduring, many of the old London County Council flats of the 1930s remain to this day, with little new expansion targeted in current development plans because of the lack of available resources and an increasing attempt to sell state assets, including public housing. The second major shift in government housing provision took place in the aftermath of the Second World War. It is customary to view the national insurance scheme contained in the Beveridge Report—the establishment of the National Health Service and 800,000 new council homes built during the Atlee-led administration—as a response to pressing social need. To some extent, this is correct; as many as 450,000 properties were destroyed following German bombing raids, but other factors also at play include demographic changes. Marxist historians such as Merrett (1979) have argued that the mass public house building program was a necessary intervention both to appease organized labor and secure economic growth. In short, government welfare programs are examples of policy makers seeking to forge a compromise between the competing demands of welfare and business groups. Many other postwar welfare state innovations can be viewed in this light.

Dunleavy (1981) made a similar argument in his study of the system built housing program of the 1950s to 1970s. He suggested that the pressure for this form of housing was from a number of sources, including tenants, local councils (especially architects), and private-sector house builders. Dunleavy argued that the shortage of available land encouraged local authorities to build high-density housing, but large building companies that recognized the potential to extract profits from the public sector exerted significant pressure on government. The government provided incentives for local authorities to commission high-rise housing from the early 1960s to the 1970s (we examine the social effects of these physical shifts in Chapter 10). In the seven-year period from 1965–1972, as many as 50% of all new council dwellings were flats, with 25% of those five or more stories tall (Pawson, 2006). In hindsight, it is clear that other factors contributed. New technologies in building methods and modernist designs had appeal for those within the state who wished to establish a collective sense of modernity and progress. Other agencies also advocated for public housing, including welfare charities, professional planning, and architects employed by local authorities. The late 1960s were the high point of public housing in the United Kingdom, United States, and Australia (with much of Western Europe having already developed significant public housing systems at least by this point in time); its role in assisting working-class households, enabling many to avoid relying on a precarious and unregulated private rental market, was widely recognized.

The economic recession of the early 1970s, accompanied by high inflation accentuated by energy prices, created acute problems for the incoming Labour government elected in 1974. This period is epochal in that all major UK political parties embraced monetarist economic policies as a response to the crisis. Welfare expenditure was reduced as the government sought to find ways of reducing public debt to pay its debt to the International Monetary Fund. The commitment to pursuing monetarist economic policies and curbing wage demands was set in motion. Welfare provisions in areas such as housing were viewed as inappropriate and a drain on resources. Here we detect the popular vilification of public housing, "council" tenants as welfare "dependents," and local government bureaucracies as unresponsive. In 1979, the incoming Conservative government explicitly embraced market reforms and legislated to allow council tenants to purchase their homes and to establish private-sector opportunities for profit in areas of welfare. The legacy of these reforms is profound when considering that in 1981, council tenancies amounted to 29% of the total stock; owner-occupied housing, 58%; and private rental, 11%. In 2013, the proportion of private rental tenancies was greater than the combined council and housing association figures (18% PRS vs. 16.8% HA/LA rented homes) and owner-occupied housing was about 63% (DCLG, 2015).

The 1980 Housing Act also reduced the subsidy arrangements by which local authorities could obtain funds from central government, forcing councils to charge higher rents. Further legislation in 1989 placed limits on housing departments subsidizing activities through the general rate fund. Housing departments were unable to finance the necessary maintenance for many of their properties, and much of the housing stock fell into disrepair. Hindsight shows us that these reductions were necessary to tarnish the reputation and capacity of local housing departments. By reducing their cash flow, local housing managers were unable to maintain services, thereby encouraging more households living in council properties to consider home ownership.

The social and political implications of these reforms were far-reaching. As better-off tenants took advantage of the "right-to-buy" subsidies, tensions between owners and renters increased. Public housing became categorized as a residual tenure (containing ever-increasing proportions of the least well-off and those with highest social needs, thus concentrating deprivation in estates in the United Kingdom and housing projects of North America [Venkatesh, 2000]), framed by its critics as a cause of social deprivation and long-term unemployment. Politically, the changes imposed on public housing were viewed as a victory for the ideological right and used as a justification to advocate further privatization reforms in areas such as health and education. Thus, the late 1970s and 1980s was a tumultuous time. The term *Thatcherism*, created to signify the ideological shift away from more consensual forms of politics that endured through the 1950s and 1960s, is linked to these years.

The attack on local authority housing accompanied the Conservative government's support for housing associations as alternative providers of low cost housing. The 1988 Housing Act enabled housing associations to operate as private-sector companies and borrow money and invest as private-sector entities. The policy was another way to curb the influence of local government (at this juncture, many of the urban authorities were Labour controlled). Devoid of sufficient resources for maintenance, many local authorities implemented measures to transfer their stock to housing associations, and in the period between 1988 and 2008, as many as half of local authorities transferred all or some of their stock to housing associations (Pawson and Mullins, 2010). The cuts in local authority housing budgets were generally unproblematic for the Conservative government as opposition was limited to welfare activists and politically active tenant groups. The broad constituency needed to mount an effective challenge was lacking.

How should we view this period? Looking back at the Conservative government's housing policies, a divisive approach was evident (for a discussion, see Hodkinson, 2012; Hodkinson and Robbins, 2013). Conservative ideologues viewed public housing as a threat for three main reasons. First and indicated previously, a popular and well-funded public housing sector could undermine the government's ambition to encouraging home ownership. Why would households take on the risk of borrowing large amounts of money with accommodations available at below market price? Second, a successful public housing sector had the capability to serve as a rallying point for organized opposition to Conservative policies. Third, large and necessary expenditure cuts were imposed on local authorities in order to fund tax cuts, and privatization programs served as incentives to garner electoral support.

Although the Labour party was elected in 1997 after eighteen years of Conservative government and sought to portray itself as a supporter of welfare, many of its policies were a continuation of market-based interventions. Consider the national strategy for neighborhood renewal launched in 1998; it emphasized the importance of individual responsibility and the need for incentives to encourage the long-term jobless to find work. The government remained committed to fiscal policies that left little scope for major investment in housing, and as a consequence, in spite of the shortage, the actual number of properties available for new social housing tenants fell. As Hills (2007) notes, around a quarter of a million properties per year were let in the 1980s and 1990s, but this fell to 170,000 by 2005.

The second Labour administration did inject funds to address the estimated £19 billion (US$29.3 billion) repair backlog that left as many as 2 million social housing properties below appropriate living standards. However, the government did not permit local authorities to raise rents for repairs, a policy which effectively incentivized local councils to transfer stocks to housing associations. Social housing investment more than doubled from the level found in 1997; a total of £2 billion (US$3 billion) was spent in 2007–8, though this was still too little to be fully effective.

The policies enacted by the Labour government failed to stem the residualization of social housing. Allocation policies remained tight, effectively making social housing available only for households in acute stress and despite ongoing high demand and need for public housing. Thirty years after the 1980 Housing Act that introduced the "right-to-buy," public housing has become the tenure for the very poor or disadvantaged. Most of what has not been sold is located in disadvantaged neighborhoods, and geographic polarization is a noticeable feature of all large UK cities (Forrest and Murie, 1988).

Rather than address the systemic problems that have led to the shortage of housing in the UK South East, governments have framed the public housing problem as one of social exclusion in which disadvantaged households live in socially segregated spaces. The problem is constructed as one in which social housing tenants lack cultural resources (what is termed *social capital*), so policies should be established that encourage social mixing to overcome isolation. In the last ten years, "social mix" has become the dominant policy paradigm, and many new housing developments feature a mix of tenures, including social housing and owner occupation. Of late, social mix policies have been subjected to critical scrutiny (for a review, see Arthurson, 2012a), and the evidence that it leads to less social isolation is scant (although there is some evidence suggesting state primary schools are sites where interaction between different social groupings take place).

The major reason why social mix policies are endorsed is that they justify the private sector building owner-occupied housing in prime locations where council housing dwellings currently exist. For example, in London, new housing developments entail the demolition of council housing and its replacement with homes for sale. Similar processes are evident in the HOPE VI (Home Ownership and Opportunity for People Everywhere) program in the United States and recent housing renewal projects in Australia. In 1993, HOPE VI was introduced and justified in the United States as a means to reduce disadvantage in inner-city neighborhoods. HOPE VI led to the privatization of public housing properties and a reduction of the properties available for new public tenants or those seeking a transfer. There were an estimated 96,000 properties demolished in the period between 1993 and 2007 (Schwartz, 2012), and the program served to legitimize further cuts to public housing and reinforce its stigmatized status. There are similarities here with developments in Australia, where renewal programs led to a reduction of the public housing stock. The rationale to justify this reduction has been "social mix" (see Arthurson, 2012b), that is, the notion that disadvantaged tenants benefit from living in close proximity to more well-off homeowners. Although these schemes are justified on social policy grounds, they are in fact privatization projects that provide opportunities for speculative investment and profiteering (Hodkinson and Robbins, 2013).

Privatization policies are the main instrument to dismantle public housing, but they have also been accompanied by initiatives that seek to categorize public housing tenants as recalcitrant and dysfunctional. Policy makers have also passed a series of measures to "discipline" recalcitrant tenants who transgress. Antisocial behavior policies and probationary tenancies are seen as a response to the residualization of the sector (see Flint, 2015). The ostensible reason for these policies is that some unfortunate public housing tenants are currently subjected to abuse from neighbors on a regular basis, and vandalism of public areas reinforces social stigma. Although not wishing to dismiss these reasons out of hand, it is no coincidence that these policies gained prominence at a time when funding to the sector is reduced. In the absence of major investment programs with the capacity to expand the sector, it is unsurprising that housing professionals welcomed funds directed in this area.

Exercises

1. What role do national governments play in responding to housing need? How can we understand the persistent lack of housing, as a failure of the state, markets, or both?
2. To what extent do you accept the view that governments have only responded to crises in housing need as a means of facing down potential social disorder and the need for a functioning workforce?
3. As sociologists, what can we contribute to debates about how best to house the poor and the excluded?

Conclusion

What conclusion can we learn from this synoptic, historical overview of the role of the UK state in public housing? First, from the late 1980s, governments have eschewed policies that serve as direct challenges to the interest of homeowners and private rental investors. Instead, policies that have been put in place have tended only to address the surface manifestations of problems that stem from deeper forms of social inequality, rather than the causal factors that sustain it. As we have argued in this book, there has been no attempt to make up for the short-fall in investment following the Conservative Party funding cuts to local authorities in the 1980s. Instead, it is possible to mark the reframing of the housing crisis as one of individual failure and personal respon-sibility. Here the work of David Harvey (2014) is apposite, for he noted how advanced capitalism has sought to recalibrate the welfare state so it becomes primarily a site for the private sector to make profits rather than a vehicle for reducing social disadvantage.

Since the global financial crisis, the shortage of housing in the United Kingdom has been framed as a consequence of malfunctioning mort-gage markets in which prospective buyers are not able to access funds to buy their first homes. The UK government's "help to buy" mortgage guarantees, announced in the March 2013 budget, were justified using this premise. Drawing upon Harvey's work, a more accurate framing of the housing system finds the market configured to maximize opportu-nities for generating private-sector wealth. The negative consequences of the system, such as homelessness, overcrowding, and private rental squalor, are not deemed sufficient to merit substantive intervention.

The symbolism of unpopular public housing serves as a rationale for privatization and an incentive for households to set their sights on owner occupation. The withdrawal of resources for the public sector is also essential, for a properly functioning welfare housing tenure serves as a beacon for alternative ways to configuring contemporary politics. In short, public housing must fail in order to justify new modes of inter-vention. This is why the welfare state remains in a permanent state of crisis; any resolution would erode the grounds for more intervention. The neoliberal project can never reach an end point in which the prob-lems of the state are resolved. By necessity, the on-going project requires framing public welfare, be it housing, education or health, as failed and failing.

9 Housing, Class and Spatial Divisions

Introduction

We have explored the importance of home to our identities as individuals and our sense of place. Even though we can view the home in terms of individual choices, where and how we live in our homes is generated by and has effects upon larger social and economic structures and forces. Our ability to afford a home is determined in large part by the resources we derive from paid work, and gender is one of many variables that affect the quality and remuneration of that work. Sociological thinking requires concerted effort to locate, understand, and find the means to act on a wide range of social structures, divides, and inequalities that generate housing problems and experiences. The state is a fundamental actor because, despite producing and managing a dwindling stock of public housing, it is absolutely central to the conditions (taxation, interest rates, building regulations, employment law, and regulation, legal controls and rules, planning systems and roads, telecommunication and utility infrastructures, to name but a few) that determine social structures in large part, the location and availability of particular types of housing, and its quality. In this chapter, we pick up on these issues by detailing the manifold mechanisms by which social inequality is expressed spatially, in, through, and onto the home.

Housing tenure, the location of the home in particular neighborhoods, and the social fabric of the wider community are critical factors that shape the experience of poverty and affluence (Friedrichs, Galster, and Musterd, 2003). Understanding these links is complex, and sociologists have made concerted efforts to understand the extent that place affects housing outcomes. Housing affects the social composition of neighborhoods (primarily through the sorting of people in housing markets into particular areas) and the two-way links between space and people. Space and place are important because the households we comprise are affected by qualities and amenities of specific locations. Variable access to essential services and employment opportunities affect the price of homes, and thus, in unequal societies, determine who is able to afford the most prestigious neighborhoods (Aalbers, 2009). In this chapter, we consider these processes and continue to locate homes within questions of social class, gender, place, and other social divisions, within the context of localities and neighborhood changes that affect the residents of homes.

Housing has long been of interest to sociologists, not least because where we live and types of housing have a perceived impact on our life chances. One relevant example is that living in poor neighborhoods is often viewed as limiting employment and educational opportunities (Atkinson and Kintrea, 2001; Wilson, 1987, 1996). This assumption raises secondary questions. Why do people come to live in areas that are identifiably deprived or excluded in some way? How do such areas come to exist? These questions raise deeper questions about the kinds of societies and nations we inhabit because inequality provides the conditions from which areas of identifiable poverty emerge. The final question we must ask is this: whether we are born or transplanted to such areas, how does life in excluded and marginal areas affect our life chances? If our educational prospects, personal health, and other risks are affected by the quality of local schools, health services, risk of violent victimization, and so on, then we risk not only being damaged by these factors, but we may also find that our opportunities for work are affected and that we are barred from resources to move to other areas. Considering our life chances in this way inevitably simplifies a very complex series of social and economic interactions; even so, it is difficult to measure or establish causal factors and effects. In many deprived areas, social support is often very high (McKenzie, 2015) and sense of community similarly robust. This means networks of social support may soften the experience of deprivation but also restrict social horizons to an estate or neighborhood. Questioning how social divisions are mediated through neighborhoods and homes brings to the fore social and political challenges surrounding the kind of social conditions that are tackled through particular social, housing, tax, and planning policies, which may affect the relative distribution of these important resources. It is never simply the case that we make open choices about where to live without regard for our income, type and location of property, and these external forces that shape the quality and nature of housing provision around us.

The importance of class to housing has already been touched upon in Chapter 1, but it is worth reiterating that although people often focus on class origins or positions, our interest in it is as a conceptual lens to gauge the social world and its divisions. Class is an analytical category sociologists deploy for understanding societal processes, change and imbalances in power, social divisions, and deeper questions about which central factors can be held to determine inequalities of opportunity and outcome, with particular attention paid to the economic aspects of these processes (Berger, 2011).

New perspectives on class and belonging

Alongside debates about the social constitution of class and inequality, there are some new primed by sociologists primed to determine how place and residence affect the sense of belonging and position in society. These new perspectives consider whether the social concept of class can connect usefully to the spatial forces and issues conjured by the idea of place and its variable quality (see, e.g., Parker, Uprichard, and Burrows, 2007).

Where we live can provide insights concerning not only who we are but also our income and wealth, tastes and our social preferences. Writers such as Savage, Bagnell, and Longhurst (2005) have suggested that class is implicated by the desire of many middle-class households to find homes and neighborhoods to which they can choose to belong, becoming immersed in the life of those locations (rather than being free-floating agents without connection to neighbors, etc.). They call this sense of connection "elective belonging."

Much recent work on class and place explicitly draws from the work of Pierre Bourdieu (1984), who emphasized the importance of social and cultural capital in shaping class identity (see Atkinson, Roberts, and Savage, 2012, for a recent overview). Scholars informed by Bourdieusian theory, such as Savage (2000) and Skeggs (2004) have also considered the political significance of contemporary class fissures and class identity constructions as a basis for our wider sense of identity and social affiliations. Individuals frequently draw upon class to affirm a sense of difference and their relative position in the social world. To illustrate, in some neighborhoods it is common for households to see themselves as working class or middle class as a way of finding contrast with others (McKenzie, 2015), and to sense this position through the way that they present their homes (Miller, 2008). These identifications with class are not the only ways people seek identity and difference; other social categories such as gender and age are also important. Some of the most interesting research in this area has explored what Savage (2000, 2012) has termed "the paradox of class." When structural class divisions are particularly pronounced, explicit class identities are often less conspicuous. Savage argues that this paradox can be traced to the influence of neoliberal ideology, in which social advantage is portrayed less as a consequence of class and more about social attributes in playing the market. As he writes, "class advantages are thus associated with the apparent decline of overt class and status hierarchies" (Savage, 2012: 147). How we place ourselves within our homes says much about an attempt to ground and display our identities. As stated earlier, these processes are also at work in the concept of "elective belonging" (Savage et al., 2005), used to show how people identify with places despite the senses of globalization and intense social change that many sociologists have been keen to explore in recent decades (Ritzer, 1988; McEwen and Wellman, 2013). Despite such transformations, people desire to make a place for themselves in the world and to choose places that reflect their values and identities through the people with whom they associate (contrast with the forms of voluntary self-exclusion found in gated communities, discussed in Chapter 9, and the kinds of loss of home occurring globally, analyzed in Chapter 11).

Perspectives on housing, class and locality

Sociologists have always viewed the home as a site for investigating how social and class divisions in society surface or manifest. There are three perspectives that have been influential in recent years: Marxist, Weberian, and Bourdieusian (for a discussion, see Savage, 2000; Saunders, 2007; and Atkinson et al., 2012). We discuss each in turn.

Orthodox Marxist commentators such as David Harvey see housing outcomes as a manifestation of underlying class divisions. A socially stratified city in which there are poor and wealthy neighborhoods reveals the wider social inequalities generated in the labor market and the ease with which those in economic power access the most expensive properties. Marx claimed that economic power was the fundamental determinant to explain class distinctions and hierarchy. Those who either control production or have skills to demand high wages have greater resources than those who don't. Marx viewed the capitalist economic system as fundamentally exploitative in that the value of what is produced by labor *exceeds* the value of the labor power hired to produce it. He saw class conflict as inevitable because the profits required exploitation of the labor force, and he predicted that social revolution was inevitable if the working class organized collectively to challenge the owners of production. Though much of what Marx prophesized has not materialized, his work provides insights into the nature of capitalism, generally, and the housing market, specifically.

Marx's *Capital* provides the insights through which understandings of housing emerge (1992/1867). Marx argued that capital expansion was driven not least by downward pressures on the wages of workers who were compelled by their relative abundance to accept appalling working conditions and low levels of pay that were then used to boost the profit rates of factory owners facing concerted competition from other producers. Housing theorists took from Marx's arguments (around a circuit of production and consumption) the identification of a second circuit of capital expansion operating through the production of and investment in housing and other forms of real estate. As we discussed in Chapter 7, these important arguments allowed analysts such as Harvey and Saskia Sassen to see the pursuit of profits and creation of housing by entrepreneurs as activities driven by housing markets working dramatically in favor of house builders and investors who derived great profits by building cheap properties that could be rented exorbitantly, in perpetuity, and with little incentive to invest because workers had few choices. The state was unwilling to get involved (though, as we write in Chapter 8, the imperative of the state to regulate and provide was also driven by Marxist arguments about the need to stifle revolutionary fervor by responding to demands for decent housing (see Harloe, 1995). As today, working people found their rents took up a considerable amount of their income and placed pressures on employers to raise their wages.

Marx's collaborator, Friedrich Engels, wrote about early housing problems in his 1845 book *The Condition of the Working Class in England*. Engels argued that the spatial consequences of economic systems manifest in the appalling housing conditions in nineteenth-century Manchester, Birmingham, London, and other cities, were a direct consequence of the labor market and the social inequalities it produced. Engels's observations remain relevant to thinking about intersecting patterns of housing and social exclusion today (Gough et al., 2006). Both Marx and Engels viewed the agencies of government as deeply embedded in maintaining the capitalist system so that profitability could be maintained by landlords and factory owners whose interests were supported by the political establishment. These relationships may be less apparent in the tertiary sector and service economies of the Global North (despite their surprising apparent ability to generate areas of profound social exclusion). In *The Communist Manifesto*, Marx claimed, "The executive of the modern state is but a committee for managing the common affairs of the whole bourgeoisie" (Marx, 2004/1848). This state of affairs generated rapid urbanization, slum conditions for the majority, and immense profit rates for industrialists and property owners.

Housing researchers have often drawn on the analytical frameworks offered by Marx, while questioning his prediction of social revolution. It is now acknowledged by many contemporary Marxists that the social tensions Marx saw as *primarily* economically based and rooted in the combined location and potential force of an urban working class may require revision. However, similar conditions are being watched closely in China, where comparable conditions have developed in recent years (Wu, 2012). The most important Marxist-based contributions to housing research include books by Manuel Castells and Michael Harloe. In *The Urban Question* (1977), Castells claimed that urban locations are the foremost sites of class-based conflicts. His contribution was to recognize the way that the state enacts policies to stabilize conflicts between different classes. Rather than see welfare, public housing, and transport systems as concessions demanded by the political agencies representing working-class interests, Castells saw these interventions as functionally necessary for the maintenance of the capitalist system by ensuring that there was sufficient spending capacity in the economy to maintain profitability. Castells used the term *collective consumption* to explain how governments intervene by producing public goods and services. He saw contradictions in the way that governments maintained social order, and he argued in later works such as *City, Class and Power* (1978) that alliances forged between industrial workers and sections of the bourgeoisie working within the welfare state were capable of exerting significant power. Castells's work stands in contrast to Marx (1992/1867), who warned that any gains in modifying the capitalist system through incremental reform would prove short-lived.

Michael Harloe also considered the state's response to housing problems and class divisions and the provision of mass housing in his book *The People's Home*, published in 1995. Harloe viewed the government's management of housing entirely instrumentally; that is, the maintenance of private company profitability is the primary concern of the state, but at certain junctures it will promote welfare programs and public housing, especially when under threat from organized and confrontational working-class institutions. Harloe argued that in crises such as the periods after the First and Second World Wars, governments put in place a series of reforms to the housing system that led to better conditions for working-class households. Yet many of these reforms have been reversed over subsequent years in what would be interpreted by these observers as the waning of power among collective working-class agencies.

Class-based contributions provide valuable insights into the operation of government, especially how powerful groups seek to maintain the conditions needed to boost profitability and assuage forms of opposition through well-timed reforms. Recent, class-inspired interpretations such as Hodkinson and Robbins (2013) portray the residualization of public housing (see Chapter 8) as an intervention in order to establish a rationale for a private-sector takeover—in other words, conditions were so bad, within an underfunded and inadequately maintained public sector, that tenants would prefer other forms of provision if provided by an unregulated and only marginally better, private, rented sector. Hodkinson and Robbins argue that by running down public housing and depicting the welfare arm of the state as inept, the conditions were set for commercial takeover and profits to be extracted from welfare. From such a perspective, the state is no neutral arbiter of different class interests, but is actively involved in protecting powerful interest groups and putting in place measures to transform the state in accordance with neoliberal ideologies that stress the value of market solutions but in reality serve the interests of profit-motivated providers in that sector. However, class-based explanations (such as Hodkinson and Robbins, 2013) are vulnerable to criticism by over-emphasizing the extent of "class" identity as an influence on contemporary housing protest campaigns. Second, Marxist explanations rely too heavily on an overdetermined account of political change by emphasizing, a priori, class conflict's primary role.

Some critics of Marxist conceptualizations of housing policy argue that the state is not a monolithic entity operating according to a singular rationality, but is composed of different interests that may be contradictorily reactionary and progressive (see Kemeny, 1981). Many researchers are concerned that Marxist interpretations are too abstract and not empirically engaged with the deliberations within housing practice; they have sought to consider in more precise detail how housing is consumed and the choices made by individual households. The most influential UK study employing a Weberian (a more agency-focused) perspective has been Rex and Moore's (1967) analysis of the housing market in Sparkbrook, Birmingham. In contrast to Marxist formulations of class (landowning class, bourgeoisie, and proletariat), Rex and Moore argued that housing markets had come to constitute a more complex class structure based around tenurial positions, and included outright homeowners, public housing tenants, private renters, boarding house lodgers, and homeowners paying off loans. Rex and Moore also noted competition between these "housing classes" vying for limited housing resources in the owner-occupied and rental sectors. They also considered how many immigrant groups at that time experienced discrimination when reliant on council house waiting lists. In their explanation of this discrimination, Rex and Moore argued that these processes could not simply be reduced to Marxist categorizations of class or the forces of production. They showed that homeowners had greater advantages than other tenures and were able to use their privileged positions to access additional resources.

We have discussed Bourdieusian research in Chapter 3 in our discussion of the meaning of home. Scholars who have deployed Bourdieu's work successfully, such as Butler (1997, 2002), draw upon his concepts of "habitus" and "field" to understand the consumer choices and actions of individuals in the housing market. Like Weberian approaches, Bourdieusian-informed studies usually attend to the choices of individuals, but in a context of wider cultural and social change (see Hillier and Rooksby, 2005, for a collection of housing studies that adopt a Bourdieusian perspective).

The legacy of Marxist, Weberian, and Bourdieusian-inspired scholarship has been significant for contemporary housing research, and in recent years some contributions have sought to adopt an historical approach, noting interventions over long historical periods, thereby drawing upon the political insights set out by Marx but also accounting for the actual practices and developments. Two recent UK historically informed studies that have appeared are Mark Tewdwr-Jones's *Urban Reflections: Narratives of Place, Planning and Change* (2011) and Stuart Lowe's *The Housing Debate* (2011). Tewdwr-Jones situates UK housing and planning reforms in the context of cultural change, in particular attitudes to modernism. He argues that interventions by the state are usually a response to economic and technological change, but their inflexion is shaped by neoliberal and pro-business ideologies espoused by conservative forces and pressure groups. Lowe (2011) also recognized the wider significance of neoliberal ideology, but his emphasis is on the role of global financial markets as factors to explain the promotion of home ownership and the demise of public housing. Lowe notes the political clout of large global industries, such as finance and banking, and their influence on politicians. The changes in the global economy, he argues, are the primary drivers shaping political developments. The examples we have offered here show how different theoretical lenses can be used to understand components of the housing system and particular phenomena within it. Marxist theories of rent and profit have set the scene, whereas Weberian and Bourdieusian approaches have helped to offer rich insights into the complexities and lived experiences of urban conflicts and home making.

Gentrification, neighborhood change, and social class

The term *gentrification* was first deployed by the sociologist Ruth Glass (1964) to categorize the choices made by many young, middle-class professionals living in working class neighborhoods in London, such as Notting Hill and Islington. Over the last fifty years, gentrification transformed many large cities across the world and has become a major focus of housing politics and questions of how states provide housing for particular groups. The dramatic impact of gentrification can be seen in cities such as San Francisco, London, Sydney, New York, and Berlin, but it is now hard to find cities where rising inequalities and house prices have not generated identifiable processes that enable higher class and income groups to purchase properties in cheaper and working-class neighborhoods.

The conceptual language around gentrification originates predominantly from the central ideas of Neil Smith's rent gap theory of neighborhood change (1979, 1995) and David Ley's views of the necessary role of consumer preference linked to emerging fractions of the middle class (Ley, 1986, 1996). Implicit in the rent gap theory was a materialistic interpretation of neighborhood change driven by wider cycles of disinvestment and uneven development, thus creating new opportunities for speculation. Although this body of theory has been modified, it continues to act as a counterpoint to Ley's ideas about the rise of a new middle class whose tastes and housing preferences led them to demand stock in the inner city. The implied economic and cultural imperatives central to each theory have often been interpreted as a sign of mutual exclusivity, though this is perhaps something of an "over-distinction." Nevertheless, there has been general acknowledgment that both writers generally failed to accept either the complementarity or necessity of each other's ideas in a more integrated theory (Hamnett, 1991; Clark, 1992; Lees, 1994).

Many households with children fret over securing access to "good" schools (Butler and Hamnett, 2011), often fuelling competition for housing resources as families jockey to access those with good reputation in the best locales. Much of this research highlights how so-called "good" schools are simply those with large numbers of pupils from middle-class or high-income households, further fueling the desire for such families to live near others who are like them and to avoid "rough" or more diverse areas. Again, these processes are symptomatic of unequal and symbolically divided communities. Perhaps more importantly, and drawing again on the work of Bourdieu, education is also one of the methods by which cultural and economic capital are acquired; school is a major resource in helping to reproduce social class advantages (and disadvantages). Many gentrifiers stress about where to send their children to school. Some with sufficient income view private schools as a viable choice, which means residence in more mixed areas with cheaper housing costs is possible; others prefer to get their children into a 'good' state school (see Butler and Hamnett, 2011). There is a premium for properties that are in the catchment areas of "good" schools, a phenomenon that is particularly evident in London.

Writers such as Sharon Zukin (1982), Patrick Wright (1991), and Tim Butler (1997) have produced some of the best scholarship on gentrification. Although Zukin and Wright recognize the displacement effects of globalization, they also note how property developers and estate agents have capitalized on the aestheticization of dilapidation to great effect. In other words, property developers comprehend that run-down areas have some attraction for middle-class households, and they often use this knowledge as a basis for advertising developments such as lofts and apartments. Tim Butler's (1997) study chronicled the tastes and identity formation activities of inner London owner-occupiers, noting the practices they deploy to feel "at home." Perhaps the primary strategy here is one of affiliation to other households like themselves in the new locality, or what Butler terms "people like us." Attempts at feeling "at home" are derived from feeling at ease with other people of a similar social background.

Recently there has been a vigorous debate concerning the politics of gentrification and the question of displacement—the process by which existing residents and tenants are priced out over time as rents and housing prices skyrocket, leaving only public housing tenants (though these are often threatened as this politics begins to shift, with proposals to demolish public housing to make way for the market provision of homes). Academics such as Slater (2006) and Watt (2009) foreground these more insidious aspects of gentrification (e.g., the displacement of working-class communities and the polarization this entails). Slater and Watt are correct in pointing out the problematic aspects of gentrification, but it is important to recognize these insidious aspects are symptoms of more deep-rooted societal inequalities that housing researchers must address. Local housing contests need to be contextualized within the kind of analyses of national and global systems of political economy that continue to privilege higher-income groups while constraining the availability of housing.

Gentrification processes certainly act as stimuli to various kinds of economic activity; the cafes and shops that have opened up in areas like London's Hoxton over the last ten years are an example. Yet it is important not to assume that gentrification leads to an overall economic benefit for the location. For many critical analysts, the primary causal effect of gentrification has been the displacement of low-skilled workers to the fringes of cities and greater numbers of low-income, homeless households relying on bed-and-breakfast accommodations (see Lupton et al., 2013, in relation to London). Commercial displacement often takes place as long-standing establishments and industries relocate either to capitalize on rising land values or as their rents become unsustainable. The net effect of these changes is almost invariably neighborhoods becoming more socially homogeneous and significant levels of social resentment and housing stress among those displaced (Atkinson, 2004). Neither can we assume that gentrification leads to a more cosmopolitan and vibrant culture as popular supporters, such as Richard Florida (2004), claim. For example, there is now evidence that many of the households being displaced in the significant gentrification processes in east London before and after the 2012 Olympics are from immigrant communities unable to meet the high rents now expected in the private rental market (Watt, 2013).

In spite of these problems, governments have been active to encourage gentrification processes through direct intervention such as the HOPE VI program in the United States and the Housing Market Renewal Program in the United Kingdom (Allen, 2007). It is not difficult to see why policy makers welcome gentrification. High house prices are a source for the collection of taxes such as stamp duty and local authority rates. With a decline in the proportion of revenue from many central governments, local authorities have also sought to engineer opportunities for gentrification as a way to meet cash shortfalls. Often overlooked is the fact that the displacement of lower-income households is likely to generate significant additional costs in the labor market and poorer health and educational outcomes. As many Western countries become increasingly divided by income, class, and around housing tenure, resentment toward gentrifiers will intensify, despite the need for an expanded analysis of social inequality that is linked to housing fortunes (Dorling, 2014).

Regardless of the negative impact for low-income households, gentrifiers have often invested in improving the stock of run-down housing. Gentrification creates some job opportunities in service industries. As suggested earlier, it is widely assumed that schools in gentrified neighborhoods improve with the influx of middle-class households. Yet the evidence here is scant, and in some London boroughs, local state schools have been shunned by incoming gentrifiers; Islington is a clear example. Furthermore, research by Hastings et al. (2013) indicates that pressure from gentrifiers can lead local authorities to redirect their resources (cleaning services, education funds) away from public housing estates to neighborhoods that are predominantly middle class. Hastings explains that the middle classes are often more disposed and have the resources to lobby for better services.

As mentioned earlier, much of the recent informed scholarship on gentrification employs Bourdieu's concept of "habitus," which can be understood as the practices by which class identities are initiated, enacted, and maintained over time. The concept of habitus has been especially influential in the field of gentrification (discussed in Chapter 5); scholars such as Atkinson (2006) and Butler (1997, 2002) examined the ways that householders' anxieties about their cultural and symbolic status underpin many of contemporary gentrification processes. In his work on neighborhoods in inner London (1997, 2002), Butler argued gentrification is one of the ways that middle-class householders construct narratives of belonging through their housing choices. He writes (2002) that "gentrification is a 'coping' strategy by a generation which, whatever its other differences, is reacting not only to changed social and economic circumstances but also against its own familial upbringing." The concepts provided by Bourdieu provide a more nuanced understanding of gentrification processes than explanations regarding it merely as a wealth accumulation engagement with emerging property markets.

Neighborhood effects

One of the most contentious debates of recent years has been the extent to which social disadvantage within neighborhoods has a negative effect on people's life chances. Many conservative critics of government policy have argued that living in neighborhoods where public housing is concentrated has not only entrenched poverty but has also led to intergenerational disadvantage. Government agencies made considerable use of this research to justify breaking up public housing under the guise of what is termed *social mix*—using programs of demolition, building for owner-occupiers, and reducing overall concentrations of public housing (often "decanting" and removing lower-income households from many urban areas) (Arthurson, 2012a).

Critics have questioned the validity of the neighborhood effects thesis (that it is demonstrably worse to be poor in a poor neighborhood than one which is more socially diverse). For example, Atkinson (2008) argues that the life chances of residents are shaped by a wider set of processes than the neighborhood. Further, he claims it is not possible simply to trace and then connect causal factors to effects. The problems that accentuate poverty are indicative of social inequality rather than specific factors deemed observable in the neighborhood. Thus, we must look carefully to identify factors that operate within (policing, schools, and other locally anchored institutions) and from beyond the neighborhood (such as housing, tax, and welfare policies that influence localities, including the increase in areas of concentrated poverty). Many governments have implemented policies to break up areas of public housing in the United Kingdom, the United States (under the guise of the HOPE VI program) (Popkin et al., 2004), Australia, and many cities in mainland Europe, despite debates concerning conclusions derived from the neighborhood effects thesis. In a short space of time, perceptions of public housing have changed from it being a secure base to avoid or exit conditions of poverty, to one that is a causal attribute of poverty rather than a shelter from the worst problems associated with it. The stigmatization of public housing fits within the broad framework of neoliberal policy making by disparaging the achievements of the public realm and valorizing private-sector enterprise. It is no coincidence that the neighborhood effects thesis surfaced at this juncture in the policy cycle, when governments seek to frame welfare investment as an impediment to economic competition.

Social units, households, and families are nested and organized within the physical unit of the home, and our physical dwellings are located in neighborhoods of varying social compositions, amenities, and dangers. Homes offer varying experiences to their subjects: of uneven patterns of resource, life chances, and norms that are themselves distributed across urban systems co-located within societies of more or less opportunity and inequality. To talk of problems like crime and its social rootedness is implicitly also to discuss questions of segregation, neighborhood social control, the design and resilience of homes, blocks and other building types, tenure, and profound social inequality. These issues continue to recur in analyses of area effects and the kinds of additional disadvantage that families and households face in such districts.

Homes exist in broadly constituted neighborhoods—places with recognized names, social histories, and identities that are embraced or sometimes contested by their residents, where such associations bring stigma and shame (Wacquant, 2008). The social composition of areas has long been of interest to criminologists precisely because these factors enable us to comment on whom we might be in contact with and how local social, physical, and economic conditions and networks might influence choices around criminal conduct or exposure to such actions. Since the writings of the Chicago School of sociology (see Park, 1928; Park and Burgess, 1967), these themes have been regularly voiced in sociological and criminological theory. Within the field of housing studies, interest in policies devoted to dispersing or breaking up these poor communities or to importing marginally more affluent residents to them has been in vogue for some time.

This is important because such programs directly push the suggestion that to be poor in a poor area leads to substantially worse social outcomes for the individual (the neighborhood effects thesis) and that such violations of household potential and social exclusion should be challenged by creating more diverse areas of housing type and tenure. In this sense, one might argue that wider social inequalities are largely ignored by state agencies concerned with housing policy insofar as these are directed at reengineering of social composition in local neighborhoods. Here the state acknowledges the damage done by offering areas of concentrated provision of public housing for the worst-off in society while denying the need to address inequalities that generate the need for provision in the first place.

There is now widespread acknowledgment among European urban policy specialists (e.g., Friedrichs et al., 2003) that deprived neighborhoods are not just the receptacles of the victims of a divided and polarized society, but that living in such neighborhoods contributes to the reproduction of inequalities and is thereby a further source of social exclusion. Yet this kind of social harm is not a mainstay of thinking about housing, though the roots of such theses are apparent in work on segregation and high-risk neighborhoods. If where we live has an effect on our potential in life, then in lieu of massive advances toward a more progressive taxation and redistribution program, housing and urban policies should be seen as important vehicles for mitigating such harms.

Precisely illustrating the impact of neighborhood effects is challenging. Though many studies indicate that there is evidence suggesting that living in a poor area has a detrimental effect on the life opportunities of residents (Friedrichs et al., 2003), these impacts are surprisingly difficult to measure in practice as net additional impacts that exceed the contribution of compositional factors at the neighborhood level. In other words, the concentration of social problems in an area causes further problems for residents, but this does not go beyond these effects. There is no or very little "concentration effect" as such (Arthurson, 2012b). The very social toxicity of many of the most deprived spaces is not hard to discern and is a feature of middle-class household angst about choice of schools and neighborhoods to avoid (Butler and Lees, 2006). Similar sentiments drove the exit of white and then black middle-class households from increasingly dangerous neighborhoods, later to be marked up as ghettos by researchers like Wilson (1996) in the United States.

These issues fit well with broader points advanced by observers like Currie (2009) who have suggested that child development in poor areas points the way to social exclusion, personal stress, and contact with violence and abuse more generally. More importantly, Currie (2009), Wacquant (2008), and various others contend that the production of large agglomerations of the excluded, housed in monolithic housing estates, is a form of symbolic and systemic violence in that it creates massive detrimental impacts on human potential while also generating more violent actors, damaged by the stressed and violent household contexts from which they emerge or responding to the imperatives of organized criminal activity that operates in lieu of a sufficient formal economy.

Housing development and class resistance: NIMBYism

As profit can be generated from owning a home, it is not surprising that many homeowners invest their savings to maintain their property. However, there are some owners who take further steps and protest again new developments with perceived potential for adverse effects on the value of their home and/or their quality of life.

The acronym NIMBYism is used to describe these groupings, and it stands for "not in my backyard." The term is ideologically specific to political conflicts surrounding developments raging since the 1980s. Used as a pejorative term to discredit opponents of new developments, it conjures an image of protesters as selfish, small minded, and reactionary. The negative association of NIMBYism and the categorization of protestors as reactionaries led oppositional groups to be careful in the way they present in public. Public housing developments are not usually opposed in a direct manner, but protestors claim that new developments are not appropriate for the area; for example, groups might oppose developments for reasons such as aesthetics, lack of transport facilities, or proximity to local schools. In the United Kingdom, opposition to public housing is often predicated on claims that it is the "wrong type of housing" and/or that public housing tenants are more likely to engage in antisocial activities, such as crime and vandalism. The opposition to public housing does not occur either in a policy or discursive vacuum, and those who campaign against public housing are able to draw upon media narratives depicting public housing tenants as feckless and the housing estates as alienating. The debates coalescing around NIMBYism foreground the "politics" inherent in housing markets and shed light on the ways that interest groups advance their causes.

The concept of NIMBYism has been deployed by academics, but it is not a particularly helpful way to frame issues. Davison et al. (2013) prefer the term *community opposition* as an alternative. NIMBYism is a term with little analytical purchase; furthermore, it assumes a binary split between good developers and bad protestors (Wolsink, 2006) and the politics of protest is far too complex to be categorized in this way. Not all opposition to new development can be cast in binary terms as good or bad. Neither is it wrong for any protest group to make their voice heard. In recent years, however, local politicians, sensitive to the short-term considerations of their electorate, supported opposition for fear of the electoral consequences. Important infrastructure is sometimes turned down on spurious reasons. It is not just public housing that is often opposed; it might be waste disposal sites, wind farms, prisons, schools, or industry.

The issue of NIMBYism elevates a set of complex issues bubbling just beneath the surface of contemporary politics: the weaknesses of local council and planning authorities to resist oppositional forms and the judgments we wish to make on those who seek to prevent new social housing. Lobbyists are often well organized and have greater resources at their disposal, and they can delay new developments for long periods. Homeowners are viewed as having a greater stake in the neighborhood, with long-established connections. In contrast, public renters are seen as transient. Public housing is likely to remain an emotive issue; therefore, we can anticipate conflicts when new housing developments are proposed.

Segregation: Housing and social divisions in urban space

The success of lobbyists to denigrate public housing is part of a wider societal phenomenon in which well-off households seek to insulate themselves from what they perceive as threats to their lifestyles. We can view contemporary enclaves and exclusive neighborhoods in much the same way. We have already noted how social inequalities are played out in the housing market. One of the features of the contemporary United Kingdom and the United States is social segregation that forms along ethnic and income lines (Dorling, 2014; Massey and Denton, 1988). Although social segregation has always been evident, new forms of it reveal the widening gulf between the well-off and the poor. The high cost of housing, particularly in London and the South East of England, forced poorer households into outlying suburbs, with inner-city areas becoming increasingly the preserve of the well-off (Atkinson and Burrows, 2015). Many areas of cities in the United Kingdom, the United States, and Australia, aside from some pockets of social housing, are now primarily the home of the rich. Low-income private renters have been able to access some form of rent subsidy (housing benefit), but increasingly we find private renters, reliant on benefits, inhabiting cheaper areas because of the pressures of gentrification and dwindling welfare payments alongside the rise of low-paid work (Lees et al., 2007).

Over the last twenty years, there have also been large-scale regeneration programs in many large US, UK, and Australian cities. Though improving the stock of public housing, programs have rarely led to more social properties being available. As we noted earlier, many renewal programs are premised on the concept of "social mix" and the claim that residents of social housing are likely to benefit from living in close proximity to owner-occupiers because of the opportunities for social engagement and better service provision (schools, health services), although many housing researchers are skeptical of these claims (for Australian specific examples, see Arthurson, 2012b, and Darcy, 2010).

Segregation takes many different forms. In some British towns (Burnley and Bradford, e.g.), ethnic enclaves feature. This apparent segregation reflects a number of factors: first, that income levels are often lower among newly arrived immigrants from the Asian subcontinent; second, that many immigrant households choose to live in neighborhoods where they feel at home; third, that there is evidence in some Northern cities of what can be termed "white flight," in which households leave areas where there is a significant proportion of households from overseas. The rationale for "white flight" is often couched in ways that are less contentious than overt racism. For example, it is not unusual for households with school-age children to move on the pretext of better schools. The selection of children through proximity to the school has created new geographies of class segregation in the United Kingdom (for a review, see Wills, 2008).

Exercises

1. What kinds of problems might a deprived household face living in (a) a predominantly poor area and (b) a much more affluent area?
2. To what extent does housing reflect wider class and other material inequalities in the wider society?
3. Who benefits from gentrification, and who loses?

Conclusion

In this chapter, we have considered the ways the role of housing and the home both shape and are themselves shaped by spatial and class divisions and how housing resources have become a site of tension in many cities. Concerning the outcomes of these issues, it is clear that current economic policy making remains committed to maintaining the value and profitability of homes above any other consideration. For this reason, countries like the United States, the United Kingdom, and Australia will remain highly stratified societies, and the built environment will be shaped by these stratifications, as well as shaping those divisions, often around tenure but also around class and space. In the last few years, social divisions in the United Kingdom have become even more entrenched primarily because of increasing cutbacks to housing and welfare expenditure (Dorling, 2014).

Also, if we look historically at the UK housing market and the interventions undertaken by the state, the major reforms took place after the Second World War and up until the early 1970s, when there was a commitment to building mass public housing (see Harloe, 1995). Over the past thirty years, however, despite both parties of the left and right achieving political power in many advanced Western nations, the ideological position of these governments has been that markets should be either unfettered by government intervention or supported by favorable government policies. This neoliberal sensibility led to governments prioritizing the value and maintenance of homeowners' properties through tax subsidies for landlords and homeowners, allowing increasing material inequalities, and not enough action to counter the spatial consequences of these divisions in neighborhoods.

As discussed, where we live and with whom has significant impact on social opportunities. Early formulations of this issue, such as Engels's examination of housing conditions (Engels, 1987/1845), viewed poverty as a symptom of weakness in working-class labor movements. The defeat of the trade unions and the passing of legislation to curtail their influence meant that the housing system remains primarily a vehicle for wealth creation and profit. Despite some reforms in the period after the First and Second World Wars, housing problems endure. Being poor usually confines our housing choices to "low-demand" areas, public housing, or poorer quality private rented accommodations. The essential issues to ponder are (1) the need for government programs and actions that tackle these conditions directly, and (2) how wider social and economic class differences are skillfully managed by policy makers in ways that deflect any culpability. Inequality thus structures and reinforces outcomes that have impact on issues of identity, aspirations, and social networks. We address these questions again in the remaining chapters.

10 Space, Place and Design

Introduction

In this chapter, we look at the ways the physical shape and design of the home influence our social lives. Understanding the relationship between space, design, and social outcomes is fraught with difficulty, with the danger of the criticism that analyses may be over or under-determined by these factors. We need to acknowledge the very complex links between the physical space of the home and the role of the wider neighborhood. As sociologists have argued, there is little doubt that space matters (Tickamyer, 2000). Our aim here is to provide an understanding of why and how the home influences our health, educational outcomes, sexual and social interactions within the home, and opportunities to shelter from harm while potentially enabling forms of abuse and violence *within* the home. In particular, we examine the incredibly complex ways in which the internal layout, physical quality, size, and the dimensions of the home shape the physical and mental health, quality of life, gender roles, and wider experience of social life.

How should we view the design and physical fabric that make up the home? Sociologists have viewed physical aspects of dwellings as less significant than the social relationships constituted within it. Much has been learned from anthropologists and architectural theorists who have shown physical aspects of a home not as mere backdrops, but as ways we configure our identities and pursue our lives. The kitchen is an obvious example; for much of the twentieth century, it was separated from the living area and viewed as a place of woman's work, where meals were prepared and then presented in the dining room. Cultural changes led to a radical transformation in the way that kitchens function in many homes as they became central to socializing and a place to linger. This can be attributed to the interest in the culinary aspects of domestic life, as one example. Importantly, much of our leisure time is now spent in the home. Public houses and bars have become less popular as social sites, but multiple forms of home infotainment are increasingly accessible. These connections between physical space, technology, and social relationships, form the crux of our analysis in this chapter.

Furnishings and technology shape how we configure our lives. Kitchen tables illustrate this. Tables and all furnishings actively shape the way we live. Social theorists working with actor network theory have argued that furnishings and material objects are not simply background objects, but actively shape the human world. Some sociologists have gone further (see Latour, 1999), suggesting that the binary between material and human objects is unhelpful because they all generate agency. Latour's work provides a radical break with earlier sociology that took little notice of material objects in the home (for an extended discussion, see Gabriel and Jacobs, 2008).

Homes are located in neighborhoods and other kinds of spatial contexts that are also important to the story in this chapter. Therefore, the second aim of this chapter is to understand how the wider design, layout, and planning of the localities around the home have impacted on the lives of social actors in individual homes. How does the locality we live in shape us as social beings, offering us more or less extensive social networks, as well as our social resources, or social capital? These two important interior and exterior relationships are vital to a question that surfaced earlier: How do we connect to the wider society around us via the discrete physical space of the private home via social networks, norms, values, and media systems? Homes are never social islands or sealed spaces that are somehow cut off from society; they are the places where we choose to live (or are allocated to live, usually the case for public housing), more or less, depending on our resources, and we select them because we perceive them as projecting who we are, a deep part of our social identity. The cost or price of an individual home is a reflection of many of these attributes (number of rooms, character and design, quality, size of garden), but also its position in relation to social concerns, including work opportunities, schooling (a major influence on house prices), the "quality" and reputation of the neighborhood, and other critical factors. This leads to a point that we reconsider at the end of this chapter, that the social outcomes experienced as individuals and households are deeply influenced by material and social inequalities that affect the ability to live in homes with particular designs, in particular spatial contexts that feed back to help or hinder our lives.

We have already considered the connections between vital social outcomes (education, health, class and social well-being, etc.) and a number of systems, such as housing tenure, the production of homes by builders or individuals, systems of government and policy, and so on. Each of these systems influences many aspects of our daily lives or has identifiable impacts on the wider groups we compose (Imrie and Street, 2011). For example, owners are likely to be healthier, safer from crime, less fearful, and better educated. These relationships are complex; wealthy groups are more likely to buy homes and to derive the wider benefits of increased asset value (purchasing schooling for their children, luxury goods, or major purchases like cars, holidays, or more house assets to rent-out to others and build still more personal wealth). Thus, owners are able to do better themselves and pass wealth to their children when they die or offer cash gifts to help their children buy their own homes. The general claim here is that social, economic, and political factors and forces affect these social patterns, but these patterns also feed back, shaping complex social outcomes.

What do houses do? The impact of physical space and design

We begin by looking at the range of ways the physical aspects of the home shape the lives of its residents. The built form and internal structure of our dwellings has an important role in our social lives (Imrie and Street, 2011). Adequate space, light, warmth, and comfort are central to the quality of our daily lives and affect the quality of social relationships in the household. Homes lacking sufficient heat, or those that are damp or cramped, place enormous stress on those who live in them. As we have argued elsewhere, poor-quality housing produced at low cost provided momentum for major housing reforms in many parts of the globe, but noisy, cold, hot, or cramped homes remain live concerns for many tens of thousands of households. Beyond these problems, we observe how buildings shape lives, without resorting to what is termed *architectural determinism*, the sense that we are products of these environments. Our homes are the spaces in which we are socialized, but the life of the household is also subtly shaped by the layout of the home. Do we have our own private space to eat, read, or relax? Is there space for children to play? Does the home allow a sense of privacy and freedom, allowing its residents to have autonomy and space away from each other and from noise and other outside stressors? The space of the home is instructive because it helps us to consider that we are not only social animals but also produced by domestic spaces with varying qualities and affordances (Tanizaki, 2001). These environs influence wider social outcomes, including health and education.

We begin with a kind of thought experiment: try to imagine a very different physical life to your own domestic experience. What would it be like to live life in a socially isolated rural cottage; a central city–located, single-room bedsit; as a family in an overcrowded apartment; in a lofty apartment on the waterfront of a large city; in a self-constructed shack; in a shantytown in Johannesburg; or in a super-large "McMansion" in an affluent LA suburb? What does such an experiment intuitively reveal about the importance of where home is, its shape, and location in relation to human settlements? Much depends on our resources, on the "fit" of our household into the space of the dwelling itself, and upon the quality and layout of the home interior. And our needs change over time, with age and in relation to our gender roles and the changing households we inhabit. We wonder where we might ultimately end up: in our own home, the home of our children, or in an elder care home? To identify these changes necessitates engaging some of our anxieties and reflecting on what kind of home we desire and whether it will help us to feel private, safe, free from disturbance, free to be noisy but not to disturb others, and to what extent it might help us to look after ourselves in old age. In many cases, this fit of the individual, household, and home is very poor and leads to a range of social stresses with wide impacts (Evans, 2003). Consider an extended family of six people: two children and a baby, their parents, and a live-in grandparent who is very frail. They live in central London in a flat provided by a housing association, but it has only two bedrooms. In England, around 4.5% of households (2011 census data) live in overcrowded households, almost the same as in the United States (4.7% in 2000), where more than one person shares a bedroom; these figures are almost double for those living in the private and public rented sectors. These conditions can be used to illuminate one in an array of stresses generated by the built environment of the home, which may lead to poor educational outcomes for children who cannot find space to do homework, strain the personal relationships of parents unable to find their own space, and deliver a more general psychological and physical series of health impacts (Leventhal and Newman, 2010).

The presence or relative absence of particular qualities (wrong size of house, lack of good schools, concentration of social problems, etc.) can affect our lives in very deep ways, but these conditions and standards are also linked to social inequalities and to questions of how the built environment is regulated in its production. State controls over the location of homes, their minimum size, or the required level of heat, sound insulation, and minimum standards for the size of internal rooms are critical to ensure the appropriate quality of homes. Yet these standards have changed radically in many countries where the pressure on governments to allow market providers to dictate sizes has led to the production of homes in many ways obsolete in relation to these kinds of social and biophysical needs (Imrie and Street, 2011). Rooms barely bigger than a bed, little or no space for private study, the intrusion of noise from neighbors performing ordinary daily routines, and related problems can remain embedded in the social practices of residents for years. Given current rates of demolition and the rebuilding of our housing stock, we require homes to last more than a thousand years before they are replaced; the built environment may lag in addressing new social formations and needs as these change over time. New rounds of housing construction with poor space and design standards may produce a long-lasting legacy of socially problematic units for which households are paying increasingly high, borrowed funds in a highly stressed housing market.

The physical characteristics of a house and its location within a spatial context are hugely important in thinking through the nature, hopes, opportunities, and impediments of our lives. It is both from and within these spaces that social life is experienced as a grounded and daily reality (see Easthope, 2004). These relationships are felt individually but constructed around large social, economic, and political forces and shaped by the particularities of national histories. For example, national building techniques influence the kind of home we live in, whether built of earth, brick, stone, or wood, and they shape multiple kinds of vernacular dwellings built as a result of these traditions (Oliver, 2003). In most countries, long-established building traditions have been supplanted by modern and international forms of architectural style and economic imperatives of scale and mass production, as in the case of system-built public housing and mass-produced suburban homes (Glendinning and Muthesius, 1994). The move from traditional to mass-produced housing in cities was pushed by the transition from an agrarian economy in the United Kingdom to an industrial and urbanized society in which private house builders erected hundreds of thousands of often poorly built houses for workers moving to cities.

We have argued that social norms and attitudes, taste structures, and social divisions, such as class and gender, affect us as the home occupants. But let us take this argument a step further; it is very easy to have a mind's eye view of a house as a detached "single-family" dwelling, the archetype of a home that structures housing imaginations so deeply in the Western world (Moore, 2000). What now happens if we imagine life in a flat on the fifteenth floor of an outer-city housing estate? What might this do for the life of a family? How might the design, location, and configuration of the apartment shape its occupants' lives (is the dwelling cramped or spacious?), longer-term life chances (might over-crowding affect the ability of the household's children to do their homework, and thus, their achievements at school?), and daily social experiences (are neighbors socially stressed, antisocial, friendly, or sup-portive?)? A wide range of factors are involved: the spatial position of the home (the city edge), the design and internal structure (a flat in a high-rise block), and wider social geography (a less well-off neighbor-hood) all come into play. When we think about housing and its effects, it is crucial to start from a critical perspective that helps us dig beneath layers of commonly held assumptions and include what may often be minority experiences and more sharply felt impacts. When it comes to a sociological understanding of the diversity and extent of personal experience, hardship, and inequality, we need imagination to engage beneath the surface and to look for the kinds of social problems that upset, diminish, and otherwise affect us as housed individuals.

We see the importance of these factors as we realize social changes can challenge the physical limits of homes. The increasing prevalence of family separation now places an ever-greater strain on the lives of those directly affected, but also on the physical stock of housing. Nearly a third of all households (28%) are now single persons (ONS, 2015), but the differences within particular age groups are illuminating. For exam-ple, the number of 65+ households has slowly risen along with the age of the general population, whereas the group between ages 45 and 64 shows greater increases alongside rates of increasing divorce and separa-tion. In line with the pressures of the cost of housing for young people, 16- to 44-year-olds are now less likely to live on their own (down 19% since 2003). In general the graying of many Western populations creates a larger number of small households with particular needs for certain kinds of housing that are more accessible or which are connected to sys-tems of protection and support (Hagestad and Uhlenberg, 2005). These changing social structures and demographic trends not only affect how governments plan for such change but also are processes that affect the everyday lived experiences of many people as these social groups sort themselves and are sorted by the housing system. Where suitable housing cannot be found, stress, hardship (paying more to get what we need), and social misery soon follow.

For many students of housing, some of the worst perennial hous-ing design problems focus on a particular type of housing. High-rise housing, particularly in relation to the landscape of dwellings produced by state housing agencies in the postwar period, has become a major issue for many sociologists of housing (Jephcott and Robinson, 1971). Looking back, such housing appears symbolic of social distress and poor planning decisions that produced an alienating and problematic built environment (Gifford, 2007). This was not always so. In the immediate aftermath of rounds of slum clearance and the tackling of deeply problematic housing conditions, high-rise housing provided a quick and effective response that was initially very popular among its new tenants, but the gratitude for addressing the problems of slums in countries like the United Kingdom and United States soon gave way to concerns about loneliness and the difficulties of family life in lift-dependant structures (Jacobs, Cairns, and Strebel, 2007). As we have discussed earlier, a compounding factor came in the form of the social residualization of public housing and diminishing capital investment, which left many locations shoddy, dangerous, and increasingly populated by high-need and potentially antisocial households (Harloe, 1995). These factors meant that high-rise projects and estates were ultimately doomed to provide poor and increasingly dangerous conditions for residents that often led, in many case, to providing a seedy backdrop for countless crime films and TV dramas.

Despite the widespread acknowledgment that poor construction quality and the absence of effective neighborhood planning created large and unsustainable communities in tower blocks (Glendinning and Muthesius, 1994), high-rise housing has resurged massively and has long been popular as a mode of public housing, notably in East Asia. Cities like London have begun the newly adopted approach of high-rise private construction to great profit and with little or no affordable housing provision. In a city that was notably low-rise by intercontinental standards of world cities, London now offers several hundred such prestige developments. Many design problems of high-rise housing (notably deck access and concentrated provision without effective community and commercial services) have been tackled, and we can see that high-rise housing accommodates many of the wealthiest city residents. The current plans for more than 200 high-rise blocks for affluent residents in London are certainly symptomatic of the new kinds of economy and financial success of city elites. The city now houses Western Europe's tallest building, which is now a partly residential tower block for the super-rich (London's Shard). Beyond elite aspirations for opulent apartments in lofty blocks (Graham, 2016), we understand more about the varying impact of physical environments by looking to other cultural and urban contexts in which high rise has proved an enduring and socially sustainable built form. In cities like Singapore and Hong Kong, high-rise housing has not been associated with poverty, as more socially mixed blocks operate within affluent urban environments and in highly developed public housing systems (Forrest, La Grange, and Ngai-Ming, 2002). Thus the crime and victimization often associated with the blocks of the United Kingdom and the United States need to be understood in the context (less in conjunction with physical problems in environments, though in many cases these are also issues to consider) of widening inequalities, economic cycles that have left poorer households at the margins, and sustained declines in maintenance budgets (DeKeseredy, Alvi, Schwartz, and Tomaszewski, 2003). Sociologists are eager to show that the social formations and economic conditions of residents and tenants is a critical aspect of understanding both the decline and resurgence of high-rise living.

Gender and the layout of the home

The relationship between the physical structure and divisions of space within the home has increasingly interested sociologists (Madigan and Munro, 1996). In particular, there is concern to understand how domestic spaces reinforce the marginal role of females, who still tend to occupy the predominant roles around cleaning, child-rearing, and the general organization of the household. These patterns have changed in recent decades, with gender roles and the division of labor shifting toward a more balanced (if still skewed) pattern of responsibility in the home. The critical point here is that the physical layout of the home reinforces gender roles and segregates the use of space within it. For example, the traditional British working-class home tended to divide the front "region" (Goffman, 1959) of the parlor or front room from the area where a wife or mother controlled the kitchen. The move to produce more open-plan homes through public housing had the effect of allowing greater interaction and visibility of the "woman of the house," even if her gender role as provider and homemaker was very much retained more broadly (Attfield, 2006).

Despite standardized designs deployed by the state and the majority of private house builders, inhabitants have applied concerted efforts to adapt and make such spaces more personalized. In an important study Miller (1988) revealed that the tenants of council housing modified their kitchens in a number of ways, despite rules preventing this. Similarly, displays of taste and the redesign of taste were often synonymous with the purchase of public rented housing in the United Kingdom under the so-called "right-to-buy" program, most notably painting the front door (Ravetz, 2001).

Considering the layout of cities, their design reflects a long-lived standard division of labor between the home and the place of work. Traditionally, the home was viewed as a place where "housewives" stayed while their husbands went to work. Going out to work was the preserve of the male. Until the 1960s, this division was evident in most British and American towns and cities. Feminist scholars such as Ruth Madigan (Madigan, Munro, and Smith, 1990) and Marion Roberts (1991) have noted how women's work in the home was deemed insignificant and provided enduring hostility and resentment in familial and household contexts. Roberts notes, for example, that traditional kitchen designs were often inappropriate for the tasks of storing and preparing food. The gendered division of labor continues to have impact on the design and use of urban spaces, though important change has occurred over the last forty years that stems from demographic shifts, such as the decline in the number of traditional family households and greater numbers of single households. Large numbers of properties are now being built in city business districts to cater to urban professionals who want to live near their work. Developers and businesses have been quick to take advantage of the earning capacity of this group; for example, restaurants, gyms, and retail shops are a common feature of these central business districts. For young professionals, central business districts have particular appeal because of the opportunities they present for socializing and avoiding the high costs of transport and long commuting times.

Gendered divisions that for so long determined the built environment of cities and the home are in flux, and new forms of work and household formation are taking shape, requiring new theories and frameworks for exploration. Research shows that many of us spend considerable time on ICT platforms such as mobile phone and laptops. The normal working day of 9–5 is also changing, as more people are able to stay in touch with work through these platforms. Changes in capitalist production and technology have dramatic impacts on the world of work and home (see Sullivan, 2004). Not the least of these is the way work increasingly invades and pervades the domestic sphere, a site that was once the means by which distinctions between being "on" and publicly engaged and "down" or "off" could be made, taking moments of respite and leisure away from colleagues and hierarchical economic relationships. Another of the most significant changes has been the huge increase in women participating in the workforce (in 1900, women constituted about one-third of the workforce, largely in domestic service; by 2000, they were almost half the workforce). Technologies such as vacuum cleaners, washing machines, and dishwashers have altered the way work in the home is performed. They have become much cheaper while routinizing and normalizing new rounds of activity and work to keep domestic spaces and the clothes of inhabitants clean and presentable (Shove, 2003). The concept of labor-saving appliances remains a notable form of rhetoric and can be found in many sales pitches, but filling the home with technology, work-connected IT devices, televisions, Internet, telecommunication devices, appliances, and so on, has rendered the home a more total environment within which we can still connect socially, perform work, and engage with others. The idea that this way of social living is some new utopia has been criticized by sociologists raising new questions about the way in which the work system, surveillant social practices alongside the use of social and other media, and the erosion of a genuinely private social self have all been affected by this technological onslaught (Postman, 1992; Gerhardt, 2010).

In spite of the rise in dual-income households and the emergence of "new man" discourses that circulate in media outlets, tasks of housework and childcare still largely fall upon females (Chapman, 2004). Long-standing divisions of labor remain intact despite the considerable changes in the technologies and the employment market. The home, therefore, is a site that shapes and is shaped by wider societal, technological, and economic developments. We associate the home with privacy and see it as a refuge from the world of work, although again this association is weakening as more people work from home. Over the last fifteen years, mobile technologies and computers with access to the Internet are reconfiguring social relationships in the home. New communication technologies serve to challenge the long-held view that the home is principally a place of rest and family privacy. The home is now a multiple site of activity that renders traditional distinctions between home and work as obsolete. The construction of the home as a place of rest and privacy has always been fallacious, with activities such as childcare, cleaning, and cooking remaining largely unacknowledged as "proper" or "meaningful" work.

Exercises

1. To what extent is the way we display the interior of our home a measure of our authenticity as individuals?
2. Discuss the paradoxical ways in which our efforts to create private spaces may undermine our attempts to achieve a sense of social porosity and connection.
3. Is the home still a space that confirms to gendered stereotypes in its layout?

Conclusion

In this chapter, we have argued that the built environment around us, in the form of the home and its wider neighborhood, is critical to a wider range of social outcomes that powerfully shape our personal social experiences, the life chances of social groups, and the nature of gender politics and relative freedoms in the home. The space of the home is critical to understanding our development and our satisfactions with the home as well as our ability to "defend" it from unwanted social intrusions or more significant threats. In this chapter, we examined these issues, focusing on what buildings not only do for us, but *to* us in the ways that rooms, design, architecture, and built form impact our home lives. It is fair to say that sociologists have been critical of the idea that space matters and have neglected this area of study. However, the vitality of housing studies relating to the physical use of domestic space continues to showcase how important the internal structure and design of the home is to all our lives. Researching these impacts has begun to uncover how social and domestic social relations and groups are influenced by the built environment and how these forces give rise to further social and material inequalities.

A major arm of research around the sociology of domestic space has focused on the legacy of poorly designed homes and structures that prevent us from realizing our full potential or being hindered in the kind of lifestyles and needs we have at particular moments in our lives. These issues must be located within the political economy of housing, the deregulation of building standards, and the social and material inequality that have produced the kind of built environment we now inhabit.

11 The Home in a Global Context

Introduction

Throughout this book, we have gathered sociological theory and research to reflect on the use, meaning, and impact of the home in modern society, and on its inhabitants, in broad political and economic terms. In this final chapter, we place and test these ideas within a global context. We ask what this context does for our understanding of the private home and how the scale and intensity of social and housing problems across the world creates new and increasingly urgent questions, particularly around the problems of inequality and human security, both of which appear as much greater challenges in this arena and include such issues as migration, housing conditions and slum settlements, affordability, and the loss and destruction of homes through warfare and natural disaster.

There is a general tendency, often termed *ethnocentrism*, to consider social issues through the lens of our own localities and nations. Much of this book has been concerned with housing as it relates to the conditions and societies of the Global West and North, as much as a fifth of the global population, whereas the combined populations of just India and China alone form around a third of the world's population. While acknowledging the fundamental and perhaps necessary biases implicit in the account provided thus far, we seek to expand what is a Western-centered housing imagination and respond to the kinds of concerns and overwhelming problems encountered when we "scale up" to a global context.

In the majority of such cases, these housing problems tend to impact mostly on the poor and those with least political capital. Therefore, inequality and poverty inevitably form the primary backdrop to much research on housing and social problems in a global context (Drakakis-Smith, 1997). Yet it remains difficult to detach the meaning of home from this context given the profound consequences of forced and voluntary human migration that affect the lives of those attempting to find a home in new regions and cities. Leaving home and the pursuit and making of new homes—whether out of desperation, leisure, or new work opportunities—unearths important questions about how societies, nations, and communities are affected by housing, its relative availability, and its intersection with other forms of economic and social opportunity. Across international borders, highly skilled and geographically mobile (rich and poor) households move in search of opportunities or around lifestyle-maximizing choices, often based around the desire for sunnier climates, lower taxes, or other economic opportunities.

To analyze housing and homes in a global context is to reveal various forms of opportunity as well as intense social distress, and it is important to understand how these networks are linked. One of the themes repeated through the book is that the economic advantages of many households in the Global North are positioned within hierarchies of economic extraction that depend on the cheap labor of the Global South. A consideration of the interdependencies and longer histories of colonialism, inequality, and dependence is necessary to examine global housing problems. In the past decade, the economic vitality of countries in global markets, such as the BRIC countries (Brazil, Russia, India, and China) has expanded the size of their respective middle classes, leading to new demands for housing of a particular size, design, and standard. In addition, the economic growth within these countries has generated large flows of investment capital attracted to the possibilities in speculative property markets in cities like New York, London, and Singapore (Atkinson, Burrows, and Rhodes, 2016). Both national and class fortunes within and between countries shape the landscape of housing and also generate new groups of winners and losers. To demonstrate, the experience of housing stress in cities like London, although being linked to constraints of low supply, is also partly attributable to a speculative market in which primarily international buyers are sought by property developers seeking to sell to the wealthiest social groups. Consequently, many homes lie empty or are rented out to other, less well-off groups in the city who cannot afford these inflated prices.

New forms of personal and social insecurity and violence in many world regions fuel the search for many looking for new homes. These groups are compelled to find new sites of home away from the places to which they feel attached and in which they wish to remain (Castles, 2003). Experiences of migration interconnect with patterns of occupation in new homes and social networks in potentially ambiguous ways, yielding feelings of unease as well as opportunities, new social beginnings, and disruptions with existing communities and kin networks (Jacobs, 2011). For many decades, sociologists have associated inner-city locations in cities worldwide with new migrants or affluent households, diasporas connected to global networks of friends and family but which are now able to communicate and sustain family-like relationships over long distances (Ryan and Mulholland, 2014). In sharp contrast with these worlds of elective mobility and the realization of dreams and ambitions, we find the plight of many tens of millions running away from warfare, appalling urban conditions, stunted economic opportunity or natural disaster (ICRC, 2009). The displacement from warfare is obviously linked to the energy needs and foreign policy objectives of the Global North as Western governments have destabilized regional locations through years of conflict and controversial interventions. Local and national responses to refugees and migrants are often hostile, resulting in new borders and walls and a bolstering of discursive constructions of "homeland" and "community" that seek to exclude them (Winlow and Hall, 2013). As economic conditions deteriorate in many Western nations, the plight of migrants and refugees becomes all the more problematic as they find themselves subject to scrutiny by working-class groups whose anger at housing conditions is sometimes directed at newcomers and non-nationals (Back, 1996; Pager and Sheppard, 2008).

A number of indicators reveal a sense of the challenges that remain for individuals, communities, and governments and the kinds of hardship and poverty that exist behind these data:

- There were 19.5 million refugees globally, 1.8 million asylum seekers, and 38.2 million internally displaced persons in 2013 (UNHCR, 2014).
- Most refugees remain in camps and informal settlements in the Middle East and Pakistan.
- Of the roughly 20 million refugees worldwide, around a quarter came from Syria (3.88 million alone following civil war there), and nearly the same amount (2.6 million) came from Afghanistan and Somalia (11.1 million) (UNHCR, 2014).

Global problems

Problems of homelessness, the destruction of homes, poor housing conditions, slum settlement, climate change, and so on, are felt most acutely by the world's poorest and least powerful (Roy, 2011). These are global issues for two reasons. First, when considered at this scale, such problems are found in abundance and in ways that can barely be grasped from a "Global Northern" perspective. Second, they are problems intricately connected to globally ranging histories of colonialism, warfare, displacement, economic hierarchies, and relationships that connect disparate nations and locales. Catastrophes associated with events like 2015's Cyclone Pam and its devastation of Vanuatu, or the event in China, 2010, when more than a million homes were destroyed and millions were evacuated during massive floods, are now linked to climate change, the roots of which are located in the choices of an affluent Global North. Ongoing conflicts, domestic destruction, and household dislocation in the Middle East, notably Afghanistan and more recently Syria, reveal the results of exerting colonial power over many years, and complex forms of internecine ethnic and social conflicts as well as ambitions to control natural resources as these conflicts spread to neighboring countries like Iraq. Such conflicts have led to the enormous flows of immiserated populations surviving in camps within and outside these countries. These cases illustrate the crucial importance of considering the implications of economic and political systems in the "natural" features of disaster and the "intractable" problems of war and conflict in many parts of the globe.

In many African states, damage to habitats caused by climate change spurred the abandonment of many settlements, with crop failure and desertification driving wider conflicts, the growth of existing cities (Reuveny, 2007), and household migration. Such processes connect to new patterns of urbanization, placing increased burdens on services, generating illicit economies and tensions within new communities (Agnew, 2012). We can observe this in some Latin American countries (Rotker, 2002; Goldstein, 2004) where paramilitary groups and wars on the drug trade and insurgent groups generate similar problems, as peasant farmers look for the economic opportunities in cities, more often finding poor housing conditions, and insecurity among people vying to survive in hostile conditions. Many analysts of housing conditions and urban violence in much of the developing world point to the effects of the trade in narcotics and the implementation of neoliberal policies that accentuate inequalities and social disparities often focused around the provision of housing: these conditions propel and fuel the drug trade and other malefaction.

Migration: Losing and remaking homes

From the above, it should be clear that migration is a continuous feature of the global economy of homes and the movement of households within and between countries, as well as a pivotal question that steers the planning for and politics of housing in many countries round the world. Internal displacement (being forced from one's home within one's own country), household education, malnutrition, disease, homelessness, warfare, and political instability are all attached to the flow of migrating people and broach probing questions about how policy makers and communities deal with such problems. The intersection of these factors, so often almost incomprehensibly huge, with rapid urbanization and social inequality in the Global South, helps to correct the insulated views and foci of housing studies in the Global North. Refugees, informal settlements, domicide and ecological catastrophes (variously mediated through political systems) underscore some of the largest housing problems globally and query how we deal with such problems. The figures for estimating the scale of such events have become a parade of epic and ungraspable statistics beneath which individual human tragedy and persistent suffering from warfare, asymmetries of political power, and persecution lie. For example, the United Nations estimates the global refugee population is equivalent to almost three cities the size of London, at around 24 million people.

Many housing problems flow across national and regional borders and generate not only crises for receiving governments (how to house millions of terrified Syrian refugees fleeing to Turkey for safety from a merciless and protracted civil war, e.g.) but also the emotional and social consequences of the immiseration—post-traumatic distress, the loss of the physical home, and educational and health impacts as well as the breaking up of communities and socially supportive networks. Displacement from megaproject constructions such as dams; economic migration spurred by the search for work and self-respect; human trafficking and smuggling that prey on the vulnerable and desperate; massive informal housing settlements generated by urbanization; the terrifying consequences of warfare; and the destruction of home are also part of this story (Porteous and Smith, 2001). These are political questions concerning resource allocation (Who should be helped and how? What is the minimum right to accommodations for those new to a community or society?), yet they also encompass human processes involving emotional trauma and attempts at repair focused on the loss and remaking of domestic spaces; affective belonging to new places following a move; the renegotiation of personal identities; and the traumas associated with displacement (Duchon, 1997).

Housing problems in a global context are distinctive, challenging, and often overlooked in media and mainstream political discourse. Instead, we are subjected to narratives that construct those problems as in another time and place, problems over which we have little or no agency and cannot resolve (Philo, Briant, and Donald, 2013). Many such issues are barely considered in the daily flow of news media that focuses on problems close to home. In other respects, the news struggles to cover problems that are almost intractable (Kyriakidou, 2014) or which would require sustained and combined action across multiple states across the globe, or problems that endure for long periods of time and about which audiences eventually become disinterested, even if they care about the human cost.

Much urbanization and many informal settlements are consequences of intranational migration (those who cross immediate borders); the process also results in larger flows of movement internationally. The familiar story here is of refugees and migrants looking for stability or economic opportunity in a global system full of insecurities and changes that compel households to abandon homes, neighborhoods, and regions that they and their families may have occupied for generations. Imagine moving your own life across national boundaries to a country, language, people, and culture you do not know. What would this do to your own life? What risks would you take to find work, new friends, a partner, and so on? Engaging with these questions provides us with some insight (albeit vicariously) about the range of anxieties and pressures that migrants commonly face before, as they embark upon, and after their journey.

In addition to obstacles such as inaction and lack of political interest in global housing concerns, local housing issues in the United Kingdom, mainland Europe, Australia and the United States, contain discussions of refugees as "economic migrants" looking to take advantage of lucrative welfare payments, public housing, and work opportunities. Some of these constructions endure because they draw upon simplistic binaries of "good" and "bad," and "us" and "them," so it is incumbent on us to grasp the lived reality of such experiences more fully. Myths of large-scale migrations and the creation of new levels of housing need and competition for jobs thrive in periods of economic uncertainty, high house prices, and recession that allow politicians to score points around narratives of exotic, foreign, unintegrated, and deviant others from foreign countries (Rex and Moore, 1969; Phillimore, 2013). In countries like the United Kingdom, such narratives are traditionally targeted at easily identifiable ethnic groups from the nation's commonwealth, but recently these anxieties have been projected onto Eastern European migrants, viewed by some as a threat to the housing and work opportunities of low-paid and socially marginal groups already occupying a precarious social and economic position (McGhee, Heath, and Trevena, 2013). Such hostility in countries like the United States, Australia, and the United Kingdom has combined with discursive constructions of difference and danger, notably around Muslim community members (Jacobs and Malpas, 2011).

Myths of welfare check–grabbing migrants are undermined by systematic research on such groups. For example, in Datta's (2008) work on Polish builders in London, she shows how individuals aim to provide for themselves, sending remittances to their families back in Poland while saving to realize longer-term ambitions to build their own homes upon return. For many Polish households, the ideal home is a detached rural dwelling that fully enables the reproduction of the family unit (the Polish word *dom* means "house, home, family, residence and residency")—something that they feel unable to find in their temporary engagement within the UK economic and social context.

Accounts of migration prove how universally challenging and traumatic such migrations are, even for affluent households moving to identifiable jobs in other countries (Jacobs, 2011). Far from a choice to simply take advantage of the resources of another community, these narratives reveal deeply difficult decisions to leave friends, family, homes, and the kinds of community support that revolve around these networks. In the desperate cases of refugees fleeing war, these sentiments are starker, laden with terrible stories of violent loss and the physical destruction of homes and/or dispersal of communities. Such stories provide an important counterbalance to the superficial and biased accounts advanced by some political actors.

Housing, wealth, and migration

Let us now consider the migration of a very different group: the very wealthy and their colonization and use of housing resources in London. Their activities are worthy of discussion, not only because they share similarities of experience (the search for home and opportunity) but also because they serve as an illustration of the ways wealth shapes housing outcomes. In much of central London, the majority of home sales are to foreign buyers because they want to invest in these dwellings for profit and because they seek London's "unrivalled" lifestyle and value the prospect of living in London's neighborhoods (Atkinson et al., 2016). Politicians usually welcome such investments, claiming they have exponential multiplier effects in the urban economy, but many campaigning residents and groups worry about increasing gentrification and the disproportionate impact on housing resources by those who can easily outbid local residents. The events in London serve to illustrate the extreme and growing commodification of housing and its role as an investment vehicle within a global system of capital accumulation. The impact wealthy elites have on urban life is rarely considered or critiqued in policy circles. In contrast, poor migrants and refugees are viewed as a drain on public resources and subject to vitriol in many media outlets.

The notable result of housing change in London is a major shift away from home ownership to private renting and a slow decline in public housing in the city. For analysts like Fenton (2011) this generates a growing suburbanization of poorer and middle-income groups as central neighborhoods become reserved almost solely for the very wealthy. For residents in even the most expensive neighborhoods, the phenomenon of "buy to leave" (purchasing a home in order to use it as an asset, but never living there) and dramatically rising house prices have spawned feelings of anxiety and displacement akin to those found in traditionally gentrifying areas. These processes of housing, tenure, and wealth changes in London occur in other global centers like San Francisco, New York, Singapore, Dubai, and Tokyo, among others experiencing massive investment and building for and by the very wealthy. These changes are notable because they draw attention to the expanding levels of material inequality in many Western societies and to the way this is expressed through housing consumption (Dorling, 2014).

Diaspora and culture: The experience of making a new home

To this point, our discussion has been deliberately wide ranging, noting the geopolitical aspects of migration and housing, but we must focus on specific nation-states. China is appropriate, not only because of its global reach (by estimates, overtaking the United States in 2030 as the largest economy) but also because the experiences of migrants moving to urban centers is similar to many other regions of the world. A recent study by Keith et al. (2014: 254) provides important data on China. In 2007, its population was estimated at 1.32 billion, with as many as 594 million residing in urban locations and the remaining 728 million living in rural settlements. Large numbers of rural migrants reside in most cities on a temporary basis. For instance, in Beijing, an estimated more than 5.5 million residents were temporary. The 2002 census stipulated that 42.4 million people were temporary migrants living in urban areas.

Local government authorities have established strict controls demarcating permanent residents from temporary workers, but since the reforms of the 1990s, individuals are able to move within China. The barriers that impede migrants are similar to those elsewhere in the world: limited social services, lack of suitable housing, and only limited access to education. The authorities have power to categorize households as temporary dwellers, and the temporary status of migrants makes it even more difficult for them to establish roots or integrate with permanent residents. The impetus for migration to urban centers is the search for work so that migrants can eke out a living but also send remittances to their families still living in rural areas. Keith et al. (2014: 248) note that Chinese internal migrants often move to cities in small groups rather than on their own. Jobs are usually obtained through word of mouth or from existing contacts. For male migrants, megaproject construction offers work. China's large cities feature neighborhood enclaves that provide homes for migrants. These enclaves are plagued by overcrowding, a reliance on temporary dwellings, poor sanitation, and the imposition on migrants of "temporary" status by local government officials.

Internal migrants seeking employment in urban China share similar experiences to those from other nation-states. Keith et al. (2014: 259) extend the work of Pun (2005) to stress the emergence of *dagongmei* (working girls) who are migrants in the large cities of China. Pun details how many young women often end up working in factories and production lines, stay in these jobs for many years, send remittances to their families, then return to their village to marry. Importantly, Pun (2005) shows us the urban/rural dichotomy only holds to a point. Although not suggesting the existence of a universal norm, the need to maintain identity rooted in home regions after leaving them does seem a common experience of migrants. The forging of a migrant identity is never simply one of disavowing the past.

New forms of ownership and community: The global rise of second homes

Wealthy elites are able to purchase properties in favored locations such as London to pursue activities commensurate with their lifestyles. Paris (2008) notes how critics of second homes flag the impact on property prices, effectively pushing out less wealthy households. The effect of second home ownership in areas of London such as Knightsbridge and Mayfair is clear. Though always a wealthy area, over the last twenty years it has undergone a considerable rise in empty homes owned by offshore residents who rarely visit them. In addition, there is a significant escalation of second homes, a feature of speculative capital and the perception that housing is a safe investment by the very wealthy. Alongside Paris', Benson's (2011) study of British expatriates living in France details the effects on rural locations in France popular with British retirees. Benson and Paris see the consumption practices of the wealthy as a symptom of wider inequalities that have intensified over recent years. The issue of second homes is a surface phenomenon that reveals a stark reality; namely, that wealth is unequally distributed and governments have little propensity to address the causes of rising inequality.

The biggest problems: Slums, shantytowns, and shadow cities

Writers like Davis (2006) expose the massive scale of informal settlements across the globe, identifying huge settlements that have endured for years, often larger than many full-sized cities in the Global North, though many in the Global North never hear of such zones. This initiates appalling social and economic conditions with dramatic consequences for mortality rates and perennial health maladies, to say nothing of education and work outcomes for residents. These settlements present enormous challenges to governments hostile to such settlements, seeing them as a drain on scarce state resources or generated by conflicts and processes in remote areas. Processes of rapid urbanization in much of China, Latin America, and sub-Saharan Africa are generated by migrations of people threatened by terrorism, drought, or economic collapse. These migrations by households and individuals present challenges as they seek new dwellings and places to call home.

In recent years, the reach of global urbanization has presented major transition; currently, more than half of the world's populations live in urban centers (UN Dept. of Economic and Social Affairs, 2002) as we can see in Figure 11.1. Population increases are just one factor to explain urbanization. Other factors can be sourced to the appeal of cities with the prospect of improved living conditions, employment, and the dynamic social life that many cities offer. However, the potential of cities to offer these amenities and opportunities to all is often severely restricted around the world.

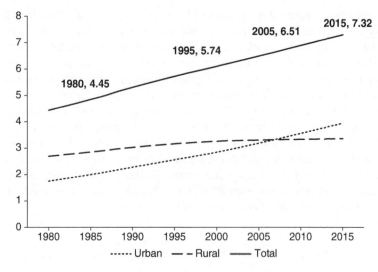

Figure 11.1 Global urban, rural, and total population, 1980 to present.
Source: UN Population Division.

Davis's (2006) critique has been used to provide a trenchant and wide-ranging discussion of the way that slums are sustained in developing countries. Contrary to popular myth, slums are a component of capitalist development. Davis argues they provide a reservoir of cheap labor that enables businesses to extract profits not permissible in more regulated economies. Governments have little incentive to commit significant funds to improve slum areas, aware that they serve as effective barriers to protect the wealthy from "contamination" by the poor. The number of slum dwellers has increased exponentially and now totals upward of a billion people. In developing nations, as many as 78% of urban households reside in slums, yet only 6% of the population live in what can be termed "developed" nations. In Rio Di Janeiro, as many as 25% of the population live in squatter slum settlements, and proportions of squatters in large conurbations such as Lagos, Nigeria, and Mumbai, India, are even greater. Slum living takes place on the perimeters or margins of cities. Slum dwellers often lack access to basic amenities such as fresh water and electricity. Some slum areas have succeeded in their efforts through political pressure to gain legal status and municipal forms of government. Davis (2006) also points out that when governments invest resources for housing developments to improve the lives of slum dwellers, the new dwellings are often colonized by well-off workers and bureaucrats. In short, the middle classes have arranged measures that transfer resources from the poor to the rich. Life in slums is often brutal and short. Building materials often consist of straw, plastic, scrap wood, and so on. Pollution, excrement, and toxic waste are everyday hazards. Davis shows us that contemporary slum living has much in common with Charles Dickens's nineteenth-century London. A decade after the publication, more developed nations are moving along a similar trajectory. For instance, greater inequality, more marginal forms of housing settlement, and increasing geographic polarization with informal settlements are attached to some cities in Europe, such as Rome and Madrid.

Exercises

1. What do you think are the most pressing housing issues in the world today? What should governments and populations in richer countries do about them?
2. Is it possible to ensure that social research will be used by governments to address these problems?
3. Do you think the world requires inequality, poverty, and misery as part of a system that maintains the living standards of those in the "First" world/Global North?
4. What are the prospects for truly tackling the world's most significant housing problems?

Conclusion

Pondering the relationship between meanings of home and the global context, it is evident that our senses of security and belonging have become more troubled, alongside processes of globalization, migration, and regional problems. Increasingly, we are likely to experience or witness the traumatic effects of displacement, disaster, marginal settlements, and warfare. In this book, we have tried to foreground the range of experiences, modes of social being, and challenges that emerge when parsing the relationship among dwellings, the sense of home, and the wider societies we inhabit. For many students, the "sociology" of housing is a rewarding form of inquiry that makes possible a critique of unquestioned assumptions about how the world around us and our place in it works. Global conditions, the sense of misery, and the fortitude of many trying to navigate and survive these conditions are nearly overwhelming. And although some of the worst housing problems in the Global North have been addressed by state governments, many of these remain, particularly in relation to access and affordability. These problems are linked to the global capitalist economy and excessive material inequalities that characterize our contemporary era. Housing problems, when looked at in a global context, appear gigantic, intractable, and almost incalculable. The reality of miserable and insecure lives, played out in shantytowns and slum areas, and the impacts on daily living, work, health, and education are almost alien lacunae to the lives of many in the Global North. Yet we can find areas of extreme violence, poor housing, illiteracy, and abject conditions there as well. The point is that it is the relative abundance of such problems in the Global South that marks them emphatically.

The problems of overcrowding, construction quality, instability, and vulnerability to natural and human disasters of numerous kinds remain a cornerstone of life in less well-off societies and those less advantaged in such spaces. A critical sociological understanding of these issues should indeed sound the alarm over the scale of these problems and reveal their rootedness in a global political economy that continues to propagate various forms of injustice, exclusion, and destructive economic policies and interdependencies.

In an age of terrorism and state crimes trumpeted by international media, the almost daily visualization of home destruction has become widespread and unsettling. In another sense, the almost mundane quality of the kind of violence, destruction, and political power seen in other countries around the world unsettles affluent notions that associate the home with feelings of stability and ontological security.

12 Conclusion: Houses, Homes and Societies

Introduction

In this book, we have suggested that a sociology of housing has not been widely considered, despite a range of important contributions from a number of theorists and researchers in this area. This book has represented an attempt to gather together discussions and research that seeks to understand the particular social role of housing, and the position of social groups within these critical physical sites. We have defined a sociology of housing as a field of inquiry concerned with the social processes that influence the experience, practices (e.g., provision and consumption of dwellings), and homes. At its core, a sociology of housing asks questions about the critical importance of the home and the appropriate concepts and theories required to understand social experiences, identity, inequalities, social and spatial divisions, and problems within larger scales, social structures, and institutions. In our view, addressing questions such as these helps to make explicit why "the home" should be part of analyzes of the wider aggregations of social life, group interactions, and important political power struggles over a crucial resource that is also often seen as a tradeable asset, even by those who live in these homes.

The sociology of housing is a field of study that is also informed by related disciplines and by professionals and policy researchers working for governments, non-government organizations, and charities, among others. This may be a factor, perhaps, that might help us to understand why the sociology of housing tends not to be recognized in the same way that, for example, treatments of the city in urban sociology have. Another probable factor is the narrowly defined policy research agendas around housing (particular a focus on promoting home ownership and understanding homelessness). These agendas are primarily practice focused and therefore often eschew deeper or critical engagements with the *systemic* aspects of housing provision. Because of this fragmentation, one of our key aims has been to contribute to students' understandings of this field of research and to present a more coherent and comprehensible interpretation of housing systems and societies.

The role of politics, economics, and welfare

Housing, as a deeply embedded aspect and mediating point of all of our social experiences is clearly a critical and exciting area of study. Through the investigation of housing we can see how complex systems (economic, political, and social) shape our capacity to attain health and personal fulfillment. Perhaps more importantly, sociologists are drawn to consider housing because it is integral to the maintenance of the human body and the social relationships and support systems that maintain it. Yet these issues can only be fully understood when sociologists seek to learn about the links between housing systems and the wider politics and broad economies of which they are a part. Housing stress generated by the cost of housing and homelessness, to take two key examples, cannot be understood without attention to the nature of welfare systems, the economics of house building, and the condition and supply of housing. In short, the housing system is made up of numerous actors and institutions, all of whom need to be engaged by students of housing to better comprehend the persistence of many problems.

Much of what we have argued in this book has been based on a view of the relationship among housing systems, markets, governments, and unequally positioned social groups vying to have their claims to decent and affordable housing recognized. These perspectives connect with ideas about political economy, which sees all economic activity not as a discrete and enclosed system outside society, but as an identifiable sphere of human activity that is closely connected to political choices and contests and to the daily life of society and diverse social groups (Hay and Payne, 2015). Yet much of what sociologists encounter in work for policy makers and the housing industry rests on a narrow framing of housing as simply an issue of supply and demand, the units to be constructed and macroeconomic considerations—such as taxation, employment levels, and income. Of course, we would not wish to suggest that these issues are the marginal components of the field of inquiry, rather our point is to suggest that such a framing fails to fully account for the roles of households, individuals, social inequalities, party politics, corporate vested interests, planning systems, and local communities—all of which must be considered in tackling the problems and issues we have set out in this book. Although political actors seek to describe housing as fundamental to the economy, we can also detect their disassociation from these wider social relations, and, critically, in doing so they construct a political narrative that is resistant to intervention and improved through social action.

If we consider housing problems at a global scale, these salient issues become even more apparent. The poverty of housing conditions and their impact on much of humanity, the building of slums comprising informal dwellings, reveal persistent problems that are not simply the result of personal inadequacy or national economic backwardness. These problems are human in their making and can be responded to by concerted efforts to address their causes and to engage with international and national inequalities that sustain these problems. There is perhaps little doubt that to act on these problems requires a commitment to help resource more humane, inclusive, and sustainable forms of settlement. Such problems are issues in their own right but also reveal entrenched social divides, notably the immense wealth and over-use of scarce resources in the Global North when compared with those elsewhere, many of whom exist in industries that supply those in the north with consumer goods, energy, and other services. Again, such questions raise the importance of broad systems thinking to better understand and tackle these problems.

It should be apparent from the arguments we have pursued in this book that sociology is not simply political science, nor is it economics in any pure sense, but we would continue to argue that good sociology is marked with a knowledge and sympathy toward these disciplines in order to be as effective as possible. As we discuss below, it is important that the social construction of housing problems is understood to establish a navigable route to deal with these issues effectively. For sociologists, the challenge is therefore to offer an interdisciplinary alignment with others also considering a wide range of housing problems.

For a sociological housing imagination

Of course, not all housing sociology is or should be devoted to macrosociological understandings of the big systems and issues at a national or economic level, much of what goes on remains connected to questions of lived experience, ethnographies of the home, the development of our identities, inequalities of experience within domestic contexts that are shaped by key social divisions and inequalities (notably around gender, class, income, national context, urban-rural location, sexuality, and disability). These investigations continue to offer enriching accounts of the home to which overly determined and economistic understandings of the home and its role have largely ignored. For us, an insightful and critical housing sociology can serve as a counterweight to this economistic and market-oriented understanding of the home as a unit of commercial supply, its role in personal enrichment and wealth and its trade. In short, the form of inquiry we have outlined considers housing as a fundamental space of social nurture, development, and freedoms. The home is more than any one such dimensional take can offer, but we have seen in recent years that to frame the home as primarily a site of economic growth and wealth occludes problems like homelessness, overcrowding, affordability, and housing quality. Although there are economists who take a keen interest in these issues, the value of sociological insights rests on its foregrounding of the experiences, motivations, and practices of the residents of different locations, types of housing, and varying household formations.

For us, a critical sociology of housing should also seek to offer alternative visions of socially just, progressive, and inclusive accounts of housing and use empirical research and political theorizing to promulgate debates around many of the housing problems that we have detailed in this volume. Sociology works best where it is not complacent and has a concern with exclusion and inequality. It should investigate problematic and politically thorny issues and consider alternative modes of social existence and political intervention. To state the remit of a sociology of housing requires us to engage with a diverse range of daily lived experience, account for a range of types of physical dwellings (often not seen perhaps as the traditional concern of social investigation, which often stresses forms of social interaction, etc.) and consider the diverse types of household within.

In many ways, classical and contemporary social theory did not attend to the home except in rather oblique ways. Despite the concerns of commentators like Engels, Addams, and Rowntree, the mantle did not tend to be picked up in Western countries in the face of ongoing problems of provision and quality. Today, as we have already argued, the deeper, complex, and overwhelming nature of housing problems when examined in an international context suggest that sociologists should seek to play a role in engaging theoretically informed accounts and investigations of these issues.

The core of these issues lies in the shared human experience of home as a binding space of vital importance; to work through notions of global citizenship and human experience we are compelled to recognize that housing problems are not bounded by national borders. The requirement is for a more internationally oriented sociology of housing that takes these issues to be self-evident and uses them to offer critical accounts of governments and international agencies who might preside over improved economic, social, and physical conditions for those displaced by war, climate change, rural decline, and economic goals. As we have argued, when narrowly consigned, these problems can appear intractable. And yet they are all linked to some degree through international and interstate histories of colonization, aggressive and interethnic conflicts, and historically embedded relationships of unequal economic exchange and dependency. For these critical reasons, sociologists are required to think systemically while locating human experience at the core of these problems—it is essential to combine abstract and grounded local registers to grapple with the causal factors that accentuate and sustain these problems.

Housing appeals as an area of study for many students because it is alive for them as a concern in their own daily lives. In this sense, we are all partial experts in the issues that housing generates for us as individuals, for those we know around us, and for what we see in the news media and our wider reading of many of the housing problems of nations and the globe around us. Of course this intimacy of direct experience with the subject also connects us to the housing problems to which we feel passionately that our communities, the state, or international organizations should respond. Both of us have taught students who have endured homelessness, domestic abuse, household separation, or discrimination. These points of commitment and anger motivate much larger exercises in offering systematic and dispassionate responses of housing problems upon which sociologists of housing hope that others may act. The link between these motivations and Mills's (1959) assertion that private troubles fuel the basis of much sociological thinking remains very much alive. As sociologists, our imaginations are critical to the identification of creative and socially relevant research agendas capable of bringing what are often concealed or invisible social problems to light. Many examples of research on homelessness, sexuality, housing conditions, and gender have been fueled by the imaginations of researchers connected in some way by their personal experience to these problems. We would argue that for a sociology of housing to thrive, it must remain connected yet remain at some distance from the whims of policy makers and politicians whose agendas are linked to short-term imperatives and the needs of constituencies and vested interests (Atkinson and Jacobs, 2009). A critical sociology of housing must always consider these agendas with curiosity, but also with a critical and reflective position.

In all of this, the concerns of Kemeny (1992) remain alive in the sense that we need to offer an engagement with social problems and issues in a way that offers theoretical depth and consideration. The danger for many housing researchers has often been that their own work has been funded by applied agencies and institutions and this has put pressure on attempts at generating long-run insights and reflections. Kemeny's suggestions were offered because he saw how it was that much housing research was undertaken for policy makers and organizations with fairly immediate aims. Perhaps more importantly, we have also high-lighted how reforms within a market-oriented society with strong goals set around generating private profits and the erosion of state support for public housing has tended to ignore and sideline work that is critical of the architecture of the financial system we are a part of. In this area, there are increasingly critical voices with wider social support, looking for alternatives and more sustainable and socially just responses to the twin social crises of ecological catastrophe and climate change on the one hand, and rising inequality and poverty on the other.

Despite many of the difficulties of this context, we can also note new forms of inquiry that suggest more expansive forms of analysis. For example, it is apparent that is there is a more theoretical orientation in research that investigates what home ownership means today within the context of hybrid forms of tenure (Hulse and McPherson, 2014). These investigations connect with difficult questions about housing exclusion and the ability of housing systems to accommodate populations effec-tively. With socially precarious labor advancing across many Western nations the middle classes of these countries are finding that high lev-els of debt and challenging labor markets are leaving cohorts of young people stuck in renting, with little opportunity of achieving ownership. Even recognizing that such aspirations are socially constructed does not detract from the fact that new forms of social and housing inequality are taking hold. It is very likely that these forms of intergenerational, class/wealth and tenurial inequalities provide housing researchers with important areas of investigation in the near future.

The place of home—an increasing amount of social research places the domestic home more emphatically in the setting of neighborhoods to make explicit the social and economic conditions that exist in these areas and their impact for residents. Social research also attends to the fact that, usually, the home contains small groups of people who form the building blocks of other groups more or less divided from others in the wider society. As we discussed in earlier chapters, investigations that explore the impact of local conditions on the life chances of individuals often make explicit how social inequalities endure. Work on housing and spatial inequalities is necessary to understand more broadly how housing operates to generate particular forms of inequality. Certainly, the concept of inequality as a lens for investigation has been usefully deployed by writers such as Wilkinson and Pickett (2009). The implication of their work is that housing remains a means by which inequality is reproduced and accentuated over time, particularly through the inheritance of wealth, but also in terms of access to housing. All of this remains a field for investigation and theorization, and it will almost certainly be a point of interest for sociologists to consider in more depth in the future.

Global housing problems—as we have already discussed here and in the preceding chapter—offer a daunting challenge to researchers. We would argue that sociologists with strong interests in housing problems should engage with other disciplines. It is clear that productive forms of social investigation often draw upon the resources of interdisciplinary teams within which health, crime, economics, psychology, and welfare are key concerns. In such a context, sociologists could benefit from more engagement with other disciplines as a base for establishing more holistic frames for investigation.

Considered at any time, sociology has perhaps been most influential when it has integrated a desire for knowledge of social processes with a concern to articulate its responses into a public environment, whether this be to policy makers and politicians or to the lay public. In its most basic form, we can think of sociology as a contextual space for inquiries that seek to provide new knowledge as to how people coexist and the structures that impede and/or facilitate this. Sociology, if nothing else, provides us with a setting for conjecture and debate as to who we are and how we want to live. With global and local problems providing massive scope for social investigation, it would seem that a sociology of housing will continue to expand and develop in the future.

Conclusion

The field of housing has tended to be a somewhat marginal concern for sociology as a discipline, but this does not mean that it has not been influential. Among the tasks that lie ahead is the need to develop a coherent statement about what such a sociology should consist of and what its focus should be. Part of our motivation in writing this book was the recognition of this somewhat fragmented position of sociologists who were interested in housing but had few benchmark or core texts through which this field could be considered. There was a need to identify what the canon of work is that might be, considered together, a sociology of housing where few systematic treatments could be currently found. For social policy analysts, geographers, criminologists, legal scholars, planners, and others in the social sciences, housing remains a field of inquiry, and these disciplines also contain many sociologists carrying a personal legacy of teaching in social theory and social research methods. This, of course, serves to remind us that that housing sociology is by no means the preserve of sociology departments and degree programs but is active wherever it is being practiced, rather than necessarily where sociology is simply being taught.

References

Aalbers, M. (2009). The sociology and geography of mortgage markets: Reflections on the financial crisis. *International Journal of Urban and Regional Research*, 33(2): 281–90.

Aalbers, M. (Ed). (2012). *Subprime Cities: The Political Economy of Mortgage Markets*. Chichester: Wiley-Blackwell.

Aalbers, M., and Christophers, B. (2014). Centring housing in political economy. *Housing Theory and Society*, 31(4): 373–94.

ABS (Australian Bureau of Statistics) (2013) Crime Victimisation Survey, http://www.abs.gov.au/ausstats/abs@.nsf/Lookup/4530.0main+features100022012-13

Adorno, T., and Horkheimer, M. (1997). *The Dialectic of Enlightenment*. London: Verso.

Agnew, R. (2012). Dire forecast: A theoretical model of the impact of climate change on crime. *Theoretical Criminology*, 16(1): 21–42.

Allen, C. (2005). On the social relations of contract research production: Power, positionality and epistemology in housing and urban research. *Housing Studies,* 20(6): 989–1007.

Allen, C. (2007). *Housing Market Renewal*. London: Routledge.

Allen, C., and Imrie, R. (2010). The knowledge business: A critical introduction. In C. Allen and R. Imrie (Eds.), *The Knowledge Business: The Commodification of Housing and Urban Research*. Aldershot: Ashgate, pp. 1–22.

Allon, F. (2008). *Renovation Nation: Our Obsession With Home*. Sydney: UNSW Press.

Allon, F. (2011). "Home economics": The management of the household as an enterprise. *Journal of Australian Political Economy*, 68: 128–48.

Allon, F. (2012). Home as investment. In S. Smith, M. Elsinga, L. Fox O'Mahony, S. Ong, S. Wachter, and M. Eastaway (Eds.), *The International Encyclopedia of Housing and Home* (pp. 404–8). Amsterdam: Elsevier.

Allon, F., and Redden, G. (2012). The global financial crisis and the culture of continual growth. *Journal of Cultural Economy*, 5(4): 375–90.

Arbaci, S. (2007). Ethnic segregation, housing systems and welfare regimes in Europe. *European Journal of Housing Policy*, 7(4): 401–33.

Armstrong, C., and Squires, J. (2002). Beyond the public/private dichotomy: Relational space and sexual inequalities. *Contemporary Political Theory* 1, 261-283.

Arthurson, K. (2012a). *Social Mix and the City: Challenging the Mixed Communities Consensus in Housing and Urban Planning Policies*. Collingwood, VIC: CSIRO Publishing.

Arthurson, K. (2012b). Social mix, reputation and stigma: Exploring residents' perspectives of neighbourhood effects. In M. Van Ham, D. Manley, N. Bailey, L. Simpson, and D. Maclennan (Eds.), *Neighbourhood Effects Research: New Perspectives* (pp. 101–20). Dordrecht: Springer.

Atkinson, R. (2000a). The hidden costs of gentrification: Displacement in central London. *Journal of Housing and the Built Environment*, 15(4): 307–26.

Atkinson, R. (2000b). Measuring gentrification and displacement in Greater London. *Urban Studies*, 37(1): 149–65.

Atkinson, R. (2002). *Does Gentrification Help or Harm Urban Neighbourhoods?* Glasgow: Centre for Neighbourhood Research.

Atkinson, R. (2004). The evidence on the impact of gentrification: New lessons for the urban renaissance? *European Journal of Housing Policy,* 4(1): 107–31.

Atkinson, R. (2006). Padding the bunker: Strategies of middle class differentiation and colonization in the city. *Urban Studies,* 43(3): 819–32.

Atkinson, R. (2008). Gentrification, segregation and the vocabulary of affluent residential choice. *Urban Studies,* 45(12): 2626–36.

Atkinson, R. (2015). Losing one's place: Narratives of neighbourhood change, market injustice and symbolic displacement, *Housing, Theory and Society,* 32(4): 373–88.

Atkinson, R., and Blandy, S. (2007). Panic rooms: The rise of defensive homeownership. *Housing Studies,* 22(4): 443–58.

Atkinson, R., and Blandy, S. (2016). *Domestic Fortress: Fear and the New Home Front.* Manchester: Manchester University Press.

Atkinson, R., Burrows, R., and Rhodes, D. (2016) Capital City? London's Housing Markets and the 'Super-Rich', Chapter in: Hay, I. and Beaverstock, I. (eds.) *Handbook on Wealth and the Super-Rich,* Cheltenham: Edward Elgar, pp. 225–43,

Atkinson, R., and Jacobs, K. (2009). The social forces and politics of housing research: Reflections from within the academy. *Housing, Theory and Society,* 26(4): 233–47.

Atkinson, R., and Jacobs, K. (2010). Damned by place, then by politics: Spatial disadvantage and the housing policy-research interface. *European Journal of Housing Policy,* 10(2): 155–71.

Atkinson, W., Roberts, S., and Savage, M. (2012). Introduction: A critical sociology of the age of austerity. In W. Atkinson, S. Roberts, and M. Savage (Eds.), *Class Inequality in Austerity Britain* (pp. 1–12). Basingstoke: Palgrave Macmillan.

Attfield, J. (2006). Bringing modernity home: Open plan in the British domestic interior. In I. Cieraad (Ed.), *At Home: An Anthropology of Domestic Space.* Syracuse, NY: Syracuse University Press.

Back, L. (1996). *New Ethnicities and Urban Culture.* London: Routledge.

Ball, M. (1983). *Housing Policy and Economic Power.* London: Methuen.

Ball, M., Harloe, M., and Martens, M. (1988). *Housing and Social Change in Europe and the USA.* London: Routledge.

Bartley, S. J., Blanton, P. W., and Gilliard, J. L. (2005). Husbands and wives in dual-earner marriages: Decision-making, gender role attitudes, division of household labor, and equity. *Marriage & Family Review,* 37(4): 69–94.

Bauman, Z. (2000). *Liquid Modernity.* Cambridge: Polity.

Bauman, Z. (2004). *Wasted Lives.* Cambridge: Polity.

Beck, U. (1992). *Risk Society: Towards a New Modernity.* London: Sage.

Beck, U. (2009). *World at Risk.* Cambridge: Polity.

Bell, D., and Valentine, G. (Eds.), (1995). *Mapping Desire: Geographies of Sexuality.* London: Routledge.

Benson, M. (2011). *The British in Rural France: Lifestyle Migration and the Ongoing Quest for a Better way of Life.* Manchester: Manchester University Press.

Berger, P. (2011). *Invitation to Sociology: A Humanistic Perspective.* New York: Open Road Media.

Bignell, J. (2012). *An Introduction to Television Studies.* London: Routledge.

Blandy, S., and Goodchild, B. (1999). From tenure to rights: Conceptualizing the changing focus of housing law in England. *Housing, Theory and Society,* 16(1): 23–42.

Blauner, R. (1964). *Alienation and Freedom.* Chicago: Chicago University Press.

Blunt, A., and Dowling, R. (2006). *Home.* London: Routledge.

Bourdieu, P. (1984). *Distinction*. London: Routledge.

Bourdieu, P. (1993). *The Field of Cultural Production*. Cambridge: Polity.

Bourdieu, P. (2005). *The Social Structures of the Economy*. Cambridge: Polity.

Bowlby, S., McKie, L., Gregory, S., and MacPherson, I. (2010). *Interdependency and Care over the Lifecourse*. London: Routledge.

Braverman, H. (1974). *Labor and Monopoly Capital: The Degradation of Work in the Twentieth Century*. New York: New York University Press.

Bryson, B. (2010). *At Home: A Short History of Private Life*. New York: Doubleday.

Butler, T. (1997). *Gentrification and the Middle Classes*. Aldershot: Ashgate.

Butler, T. (2002). Thinking global but acting local: The middle classes in the city, *Sociological Research*, 7(3), online at http://www.socresonline.org.uk/7/3/butler.html.

Butler, T., and Hamnett, C. (2011). Location, education: Place, choice and constraint in London. *Children's Geographies*, 9(1): 35–48.

Butler, T., and Lees, L. (2006). Super-gentrification in Barnsbury, London: Globalization and gentrifying global elites at the neighbourhood level. *Transactions of the British Institute of Geographers*, 31(4): 467–87.

Callon, M. (1986). Some elements of a sociology of translation. In: J. Law (Ed.), *Power, Action and Belief. Sociological Monograph 34*. London: Routledge.

Castells, M. (1977). *The Urban Question*. London: Edward Arnold.

Castells, M. (1978). *City, Class and Power*. Houndsmill: Macmillan.

Castles, S. (2003). Towards a sociology of forced migration and social transformation. *Sociology*, 37(1): 13–34.

Chapman, T. (2004). *Gender and Domestic Life: Changing Practices in Families and Households*. Basingstoke: Palgrave Macmillan.

Clapham, D. (2002). Housing pathways: A post modern analytical framework. *Housing, Theory and Society*, 19(2): 57–68.

Clark, E. (1992). On gaps in gentrification theory. *Housing Studies*, 7(1): 16–26.

Cloke, P., May, J., and Johnsen, S. (2010). *Swept Up Lives? Re-envisioning the Homeless City*. New York: John Wiley & Sons.

Cohen, L., and Felson, M. (1979). Social change and crime rate trends: A routine activity approach. *American Sociological Review*, 44(4): 588–608.

Cohen, S. (1988). *Against Criminology*. Piscataway, NJ: Transaction Publishers.

Colic-Peisker, V., and Johnson, G. (2012). Liquid life, solid homes: Young people, class and homeownership in Australia. *Sociology*, 46(4): 728–43.

Cook, N., Smith, S., and Searle, B. (2013). Debted objects: Homemaking in an era of mortgage enabled consumption. *Housing, Theory and Society*, 30(3): 293–311.

CoreLogic (2015). *National Foreclosure Report*. Irvine: CoreLogic.

Courchane, M., and Kogut, D. (2012). Subprime mortgages. In S. Smith, M. Elsinga, L. Fox O'Mahony, S. Ong, S. Wachter, and M. Eastaway (Eds.), *The International Encyclopedia of Housing and Home* (pp. 51–9). Amsterdam: Elsevier.

Cresswell, T. (2006). *On the Move: Mobility in the Modern World*. London: Routledge.

Croft, J. (2001). 'A risk' or 'at risk'? Reconceptualising housing debt in a risk welfare society. *Housing Studies*, 16(6): 737–53.

Currie, E. (2005). *The Road to Whatever: Middle-class Culture and the Crisis of Adolescence*. New York: Macmillan.

Currie, E. (2009). *The Roots of Danger: Violent Crime in Global Perspective*. London: Prentice Hall.

Dalla Costa, M., and James, S. (1973). *The Power of Women and the Subversion of the Community*. Bristol: Falling Wall.

Darcy, M. (2010). De-concentration of disadvantage and mixed income housing: A critical discourse approach, *Housing, Theory and Society*, 27(1): 1–22.

Datta, A. (2008). Building differences: Material geographies of home(s) among Polish builders in London. *Transactions of the Institute of British Geographers*, 33(4): 518–31.

Davis, M. (2006). *Planet of Slums*. London: Verso.

Davison, G., Legacy, C., Liu, E., Han, H., Phibbs, P., Nouwelant, R., Darcy, M., and Piracha, A. (2013). Understanding and addressing community opposition to affordable housing development, AHURI Final Report No 211. Melbourne: Australian Housing and Urban Research Institute.

Department of Communities and Local Government (DCLG). (2015). *Trends in Tenure Data*. London: DCLG.

DeKeseredy, W., Alvi, S., Schwartz, M., and Tomaszewski, A. (2003). *Under Siege: Poverty and Crime in a Public Housing Community*. Lanham, MD: Lexington Books.

Dorling, D. (2014). *All That Is Solid: How the Great Housing Disaster Defines Our Times, and What We Can Do About It*. London: Penguin.

Drakakis-Smith, D. (1997). Third World cities: Sustainable Urban Development III—Basic Needs and Human Rights. *Urban Studies*, 34(5–6): 797–823.

Duchon, D. A. (1997). Home is where you make it: Hmong refugees in Georgia. *Urban Anthropology and Studies of Cultural Systems and World Economic Development*, 26(1): 71–92.

Dunleavy, P. (1981). *The Politics of Mass Housing 1945–1975: A Study of Corporate Power and Professional Influence in the Welfare State*. Oxford: Clarendon Press.

Dupuis, A., and Thorns, D. C. (2002). Home, home ownership and the search for ontological security. *Sociological Review*, 46(1): 24–47.

Dupuis, A., and Thorns, D. C. (1996). Meanings of home for older home owners. *Housing Studies*, 11(4): 485–501.

Duyvendak, J. W. (2011). *The Politics of home: Belonging and Nostalgia in Europe and the United States*. Basingstroke: Palgrave Macmillan.

Easthope, H. (2004). A place called home. *Housing, Theory and Society*, 21(3): 128–38.

Eisenstein, Z. (1999). Constructing a theory of capitalist patriarchy and socialist feminism. *Critical Sociology*, 25(2–3): 196–220.

Elliott, J., and Pais, J. (2006). Race, class, and Hurricane Katrina: Social differences in human responses to disaster. *Social Science Research*, 35(2): 295–321.

Engels, F. (1987/1845). *The Condition of the Working Class in England*. New York: Penguin Books.

Evans, G. W. (2003). The built environment and mental health. *Journal of Urban Health*, 80(4): 536–55.

Federal Bureau of Investigation (FBI). (2010). Uniform Crime Reports: Burglary. Available at https://www.fbi.gov/about-us/cjis/ucr/crime-in-the-u.s/2010/crime-in-the-u.s.-2010/property-crime/burglarymain.

Fenton, A. (2011). *Housing Benefit Reform and the Spatial Segregation of Low-Income Households in London*. London: LSE e-prints.

Fields, D. J. (2013). *From Property Abandonment to Predatory Equity: Writings on Financialization and Urban Space in New York City*. New York: City University of New York.

Fisher, M. (2009). *Capitalist Realism: Is There No Alternative?* Hampshire: John Hunt Publishing.

Fitzpatrick, S. (2005). Explaining homelessness: A critical realist perspective. *Housing, Theory and Society*, 22(1): 1–17.

Flint, J., (2015). Housing and the realignment of urban-spatial contracts. *Housing, Theory and Society*, 32(1): 39–53.

Flint, J., and Nixon, J. (2006). Governing neighbours: Anti-social behaviour orders and new forms of regulating conduct in the UK. *Urban Studies*, 43: 939–55.

Florida, R. (2004). *Cities and the Creative Class*. New York: Routledge.

Foley, D. (1980). The sociology of housing. *Annual Review of Sociology*, 6 (1980): 457–78.

Forced Migration Review. (2004). *Forced Migration Review No 20*, http://www.fmreview.org/FMRpdfs/FMR20/FMR2021.pdf (accessed 1 April 2015).

Ford, J., Burrows, R., and Nettleton, S. (2001). *Home Ownership in a Risk Society: A Social Analysis of Mortgage Arrears and Possessions*. Plainsboro, NJ: Associated University Presses.

Forrest, R., and Hirayama, Y. (2014). The financialisation of the social project: Embedded liberalism, neoliberalism and home ownership. *Urban Studies*, 52(2): 233–44.

Forrest, R., La Grange, A., and Ngai-Ming, Y. (2002). Neighbourhood in a high rise, high density city: Some observations on contemporary Hong Kong. *The Sociological Review*, 50(2): 215–40.

Forrest, R., and Murie, A. (1988). *Selling the Welfare State: The Privatisation of Public Housing*. London: Routledge.

Fox O'Mahony, L. (2007). *Conceptualising Home: Theories, Laws and Policies*. Oxford: Hart Publishing.

Fox O'Mahony, L. (2012). Meanings of home. In S. Smith, M. Elsinga, L. Fox O'Mahony, S. Ong, S. Wachter, and M. Eastaway (Eds.), *Encyclopedia of House and Home*. Amsterdam: Elsevier, 221–31.

Fox, L. (2002). The meaning of home: A chimerical concept or a legal challenge? *Journal of Law and Society*, 29(2): 580–610.

Franklin, A. (2012). A lonely society? Loneliness and liquid modernity in Australia. *Australian Journal of Social Issues*, 47(1): 11–28.

Friedrichs, J., Galster, G., and Musterd, S. (2003). Neighbourhood effects on social opportunities: The European and American research and policy context. *Housing Studies*, 18(6): 797–806.

Furlong, A. (2008). The Japanese hikikomori phenomenon: Acute social withdrawal among young people. *The Sociological Review*, 56(2): 309–25.

Gabriel, M., and Jacobs, K. (2008). The post-social turn: Challenges for housing research, *Housing Studies*, 23(4): 527–40.

Gadd, D., and Jefferson, T. (2007). *Psychosocial Criminology*. London: Sage.

Gerhardt, S. (2010). *The Selfish Society: How We All Forgot to Love One Another and Made Money Instead*. New York: Simon & Schuster.

Giddens, A. (1991). The self: Ontological security and existential anxiety. In A. Giddens (Ed.), *Modernity and Self-Identity: Self and Society in the Late Modern Age*. Cambridge: Polity.

Gifford, R. (2007). The consequences of living in high-rise buildings. *Architectural Science Review*, 50(1): 2–17.

Gillis, S., and Hollows, J. (Eds.), (2008). *Feminism, Domesticity and Popular Culture*. London: Routledge.

Glass, R. (1964). Introduction. In R. Glass (Ed.), *London: Aspects of Change*. Centre for Urban Studies Report No. 3 (pp. xiii–xlii). London: MacGibbon and Kee.

Glendinning, M., and Muthesius, S. (1994). *Tower Block: Modern Public Housing in England, Scotland, Wales and Northern Ireland*. New Haven, CT and London: Yale University Press.

Goffman, E. (1959). *The Presentation of Self in Everyday Life*. Garden City, NY: Anchor.

Goldsack, A. (1999). A haven in a heartless world? Women and domestic violence. In T. Chapman and J. Hockey (Eds.), *Ideal Home? Social Change and Domestic Life* (pp. 121–32). London: Routledge.

Goldstein, D. M. (2004). *The Spectacular City: Violence and Performance in Urban Bolivia*. Durham, NC: Duke University Press.

Gorman-Murray, A. (2008). Masculinity and the home: A critical review and conceptual framework. *Australian Geographer*, 29(3): 367–79.

Gorman-Murray, A. (2012). Experiencing home: Sexuality. In S. Smith, M. Elsinga, L. Fox O'Mahony, S. Ong, S. Wachter, and M. Eastaway (Eds.), *International Encyclopedia of Housing and Home* (pp. 152–7). Amsterdam: Elsevier.

Gorz, A. (1982). *Farewell to the Working Class: An Essay on Post-Industrial Socialism*. London: Pluto.

Gotham, K. (2011). Cascading crisis: The crisis policy nexus and the restructuring of the US housing finance system. *Critical Sociology*, 38(1): 107–22.

Gough, J., Eisenschitz, A., and McCulloch, A. (2006). *Spaces of Social Exclusion*. London: Routledge.

Graham, S. (2015). *Vertical: The City From Above and Below*. London: Verso.

Hagestad, G. O., and Uhlenberg, P. (2005). The social separation of old and young: A root of ageism. *Journal of Social Issues*, 61(2): 343–60.

Hamnett, C. (1991). The blind men and the elephant—the explanation of gentrification. *Transactions of the Institute of British Geographers*, 16(2): 173–89.

Hamnett, C. (2003). Gentrification and the middle-class remaking of inner London, 1961–2001. *Urban Studies*, 40(12): 2401–26.

Hamnett, C. (2005). *Winners and Losers: Home Ownership in Modern Britain*. London: Routledge.

Harloe, M. (1995). *The People's Home: Social Rented Housing in Europe and America*. Oxford: Blackwell.

Harvey, D. (1973/2009). *Social Justice and the City*, rev. ed. Athens and London: University of Georgia Press.

Harvey, D. (1976). Labour, capital, and class struggle around the built environment in advanced capitalist societies. *Politics and Society*, 6, 265–95.

Harvey, D. (2008). The right to the city. *New Left Review*, 58: 23–40.

Harvey, D. (2010). *The Enigma of Capital: And the Crises of Capitalism*. London: Profile Books.

Harvey, D. (2014). *Seventeen Contradictions and the End of Capitalism*. London: Profile Books.

Hastings, A., and Dean, J. (2003). Challenging images: Tackling stigma through estate regeneration. *Policy & Politics*, 31(2): 171–84.

Hastings, A., Bailey, N., Bramley, G., Croudace, R., and Watkins, D. (2013). "Managing" the middle-classes: Urban managers, public services and the response to middle-class capture. *Local Government Studies*, 40(2): 203–23.

Hay, C., and Payne, A. (Eds.), (2015). *Civic Capitalism*. Cambridge: Polity Press.

Hayden, D. (2009). *Building Suburbia: Green Fields and Urban Growth, 1820–2000*. New York: Vintage.

Heinen, J. (1997). Public/private: Gender—social and political citizenship in Eastern Europe. *Theory and Society*, 26(4): 577–97.

Heywood, F., and Naz, M. (1990). *Clearance: The View from the Streets*. London: Community Forum.

Highmore, B. (2014). *The Great Indoors: At Home in the Modern British House*. London: Profile Books.

Hillier, J., and Rooksby, E. (2005). *Habitus: A Sense of Place*. Aldershot: Ashgate.

Hills, J. (2007). Ends and means: The future roles of social housing in England, *Case Report No. 34*. London: LSE.

Hiscock, R., Kearns, A., Macintyre, S., and Ellaway, A. (2010). Ontological security and psycho-social benefits from the home: Qualitative evidence on issues of tenure. *Housing, Theory and Society*, 18(1–2): 50–66.

Hodkinson, S. (2012). The return of the housing question, *Ephemera*, 12(4): 423–44.

Hodkinson, S., and Robbins, G. (2013). The return of class war conservatism? Housing under the UK coalition government. *Critical Social Policy*, 33(1): 57–77.

Hope, T. (2000). Inequality and the clubbing of private security. In T. Hope and R. Sparks (Eds.), *Crime, Risk and Insecurity* (pp. 83–106). London: Routledge.

Hulse, K., and Mcpherson, A. (2014). Exploring dual housing tenure status as a household response to demographic, social and economic change. *Housing Studies*, 29(8): 1028–44.

International Committee of the Red Cross (ICRC). (2009). *Internal Displacement in Armed Conflict: Facing Up to the Challenges*. Geneva: ICR.

Imrie, R., and Street, E. (2011). *Architectural Design and Regulation*. New York: John Wiley & Sons.

Irigaray, L. (1985). *This Sex Which Is Not One*. Ithaca, NY: Cornell University Press.

Jacobs, J., and Smith, S. (2008). Living room: Rematerialising home. *Environment and Planning* A, 40(3): 515–19.

Jacobs, J. M., Cairns, S., and Strebel, I. (2007). A tall storey... but, a fact just the same: The Red Road high-rise as a black box. *Urban Studies*, 44(3): 609–29.

Jacobs, K. (2011). *Experience and Representation: Contemporary Perspectives on Migration in Australia*. Aldershot: Ashgate.

Jacobs, K., Berry, M., and Dalton, T. (2013). A dead and broken system? "Insider" views of the future role of Australian public housing. *International Journal of Housing Policy*, 13(2): 183–201.

Jacobs, K., Kemeny, J., and Manzi, T. (1999). The struggle to define homelessness: A constructivist approach. In S. Hutson and D. Clapham (Eds.), *Homelessness: Public Policies and Private Troubles* (pp. 11–25). London: Cassells.

Jacobs, K., and Malpas, J. (Eds.), (2011). *Ocean to Outback: Cosmopolitanism in Contemporary Australia*. Crawley WA: UWA Publishing.

Jarvis, H. (1999). The tangled webs we weave: Household strategies to co-ordinate home and work. *Work, Employment and Society*, 13(2): 225–47.

Jephcott, P., and Robinson, H. (1971). *Homes in High Flats*. Edinburgh: Oliver and Boyd.

Jones, C., and Richardson, H. (2014). Housing markets and policy in the UK and the USA: A review of the differential impact of the global housing crisis. *International Journal of Housing Markets and Analysis*, 7(1): 129–44.

Jones, G., and Thomas De Benitez, S. (2012). Homeless people: Street children in Mexico. In S. Smith, M. Elsinga, L. Fox O'Mahony, S. Ong, S. Wachter, and M. Eastaway (Eds.), *Encyclopaedia of Housing and Home* (pp. 138–43). Amsterdam: Elsevier.

Keith, M., Lash, S., Arnoldi, J., and Rooker, T. (2014). *China: Constructing Capitalism*. London: Routledge.

Kemeny, J. (1981). *The Myth of Homeownership*. London: Routledge.

Kemeny, J. (1983). *The Great Australian Nightmare: A Critique of the Home-Ownership Ideology*. Melbourne: Georgian House.

Kemeny, J. (1992). *Housing and Social Theory*. London: Routledge.

King, P. (2004). *Private Dwelling: Contemplating the Use of Housing*. New York: Psychology Press.

Kleinman, M. (1998). Policies: Convergence or collapse. In M. Kleinman, W. Matznetter, and M. Stephens (Eds.), *European Integration and Housing Policy* (pp. 239–55). London: Routledge.

Kyriakidou, M. (2014). Media witnessing: Exploring the audience of distant suffering. *Media, Culture & Society*, 37(2): 215–31.

Lanchester, J. (2010). *Whoops*. London: Allen Lane.

Lanchester, J. (2012). *Capital*, London: Faber and Faber.

Langley, P. (2008). *The Everyday Life of Global Finance: Saving and Borrowing in Anglo-America*. Oxford: Oxford University Press.

Lash, S. (1999). *Another Modernity, A Different Rationality*. Oxford: Blackwell.

Latour, B. (1991). The Berlin key or how to do things with words. In P. Graves-Brown (Eds.), *Matter, Materiality and Modern Culture*. (pp. 10–21). London: Routledge.

Latour, B. (1993). *We Have Never Been Modern*. Hemel Hempstead: Harvester Wheatsheaf.

Latour, B. (1999). On recalling ANT. *The Sociological Review*, 47(1): 15–25.

Law, J. (1992). Notes on the theory of the actor network: Ordering, strategy, and heterogeneity. *Systems Practice* 5(4): 379–93.

Lees, L. (1994). Rethinking gentrification: Beyond the positions of economics or culture. *Progress in Human Geography*, 18(2): 137–50.

Lees, L., Slater, T., and Wyly, E. (2007). *Gentrification*. London: Routledge.

LeGates, R., and Hartman, C. (1986). The anatomy of displacement in the United States. In N. Smith and P. Williams (Eds.), *Gentrification of the City*. London: Unwin Hyman.

Lemanski, C. (2011). Moving up the ladder or stuck on the bottom rung? Homeownership as a solution to poverty in urban South Africa. *International Journal of Urban and Regional Research*, 35(1): 57–77.

Letiecq, B. L., and Koblinsky, S. A. (2004). Parenting in violent neighborhoods: African American fathers share strategies for keeping children safe. *Journal of Family Issues*, 25(6): 715–34.

Leventhal, T., and Newman, S. (2010). Housing and child development. *Children and Youth Services Review*, 32(9): 1165–74.

Ley, D. (1986). Alternative explanations for inner-city gentrification: A Canadian assessment. *Annals of the Association of American Geographers*, 76(4): 521–35.

Ley, D. (1996). *The New Middle Class and the Remaking of the Central City*. Oxford: Oxford University Press.

Lipovetsky, G., and Charles, S. (2005). *Hypermodern Times*. Cambridge: Polity.

Loewy, R., and Snaith, W. (1967). *The Motivations Towards Homes and Housing*. New York: Project Home Committee.

Lowe, S. (2011). *The Housing Debate*. Bristol: Policy Press.

Lund, B. (2011). *Understanding Housing Policy*. Bristol: Policy Press.

Lupton, R., Vizard, P., Fitzgerald, A., Fenton, A., Gambaro, L., and Cunliffe, J. (2013). Prosperity, poverty and inequality in London 2000/01–2010/11, Social Policy in Cold Climate: Research Report 3. London: CASE, LSE.

Madigan, R., and Munro, M. (1996). House beautiful: Style and consumption in the home. *Sociology*, 30(1): 41–57.

Madigan, R., Munro, M., and Smith, S. (1990). Gender and the meaning of the home. *International Journal of Urban and Regional Research*, 14: 625–47.

Mallet, S. (2006). Understanding the home: A critical review of the literature. *The Sociological Review*, 52(1): 62–89.

Malpass, P. (2005). *Housing and the Welfare State*. Basingstoke: Palgrave Macmillan.

Malpass, P. (2008). Housing and the new welfare state: Wobbly pillar or cornerstone? *Housing Studies*, 23(1): 1–19.

Malpass, P., and Murie, A. (1987). *Housing Policy and Practice*. London: Routledge.

Marcuse, P. (1986). Abandonment, gentrification and displacement: The linkages in New York City. In N. Smith and P. Williams (Eds.), *Gentrification of the City*. London: Unwin Hyman.

Marsh, A., and Gibb, K. (2011). Uncertainty, expectations and behavioural aspects of housing market choices. *Housing, Theory and Society*, 28(3): 215–35.

Marston, G. (2004). *Social Policy and Discourse Analysis: Policy Change in Public Housing*. Aldershot: Ashgate.

Marx, K. (2004/1848). *The Communist Manifesto*. Harmondsworth: Penguin.

Marx. K. (1992/1867). *Capital: A Critique of Political Economy*. Harmondsworth: Penguin.

Massey, D. B. (1995). *Spatial Divisions of Labor: Social Structures and the Geography of Production, 2nd ed.* London: Routledge.

Massey, D., and Denton, N. (1988). The dimensions of residential segregation. *Social Forces*, 67: 281–315.

McEwen, R., and Wellman, B. (2013). Relationships, community, and networked individuals. In R. Teigland and D. Powers (Eds.), *The Immersive Internet: Reflections on the Entangling of the Virtual with Society, Politics and the Economy* (pp. 168–79). London: Palgrave Macmillan.

McGhee, D., Heath, S., and Trevena, P. (2013). Post-accession Polish migrants–their experiences of living in "low-demand" social housing areas in Glasgow. *Environment and Planning A*, 45(2): 329–43.

McKee, K. (2009). Post-Foucauldian Governmentality: What does it offer critical social policy analysis? *Critical Social Policy*, 29(3): 465–86.

McKenzie, L. (2015). *Getting By: Estates, class and culture in austerity Britain*. Bristol: Policy Press.

Merritt, S. (1979). *State Housing in Britain*. London: Routledge, Kegan Paul.

Merton, R. K. (1948). The social psychology of housing. In W. Dennis et al. (Eds.), *Current Trends in Social Psychology* (pp. 163–217). Pittsburgh: University of Pittsburgh Press.

Merton, R., West, P., Jahoda, M., and Selvin, H. (Eds.), (1951). Social policy and social research in Housing. *Journal of Social Issues*, 7: 1–187.

Michael, M., and Garver, W. (2009). Home beyond home. *Space and Culture*, 12(3): 359–70.

Miller, D. (1987). *Material Culture and Mass Consumption*. Oxford: Blackwell.

Miller, D. (1988). Appropriating the state on the council estate, *Man*, 23(3): 353–72.

Miller, D. (2008). *The Comfort of Things*. Cambridge: Polity.

Miller, D. (2010). *Stuff*. Cambridge: Polity.

Miller, D. (Ed.). (2001). *Home Possessions: Material Culture Behind Closed Doors*. London: Berg.

Mills, C. Wright (1959). *The Sociological Imagination*. New York: Oxford University Press.

Moore, J. (2000). Placing home in context. *Journal of environmental psychology*, 20(3): 207–17.

Morgan, D. H. J. (2013). Socialization and the family. In B. Cosin and M. Hales (Eds.), *Families, Education and Social Differences* (p. 4). London: Routledge/Open University Press.

Murdoch, J. (1998). The spaces of actor-network theory. *Geoforum*, 29(4): 357–74.

Newman, O. (1972). *Defensible Space: Crime Prevention Through Urban Design*. New York: Macmillan.

Nuttgens, P. (1989). *The Home Front: Housing the People 1840–1990*. London: BBC Books.

Oakley, A. (1974a). *Housewife*. London: Allen Lane.

Oakley, A. (1974b). *The Sociology of Housework*. London: Martin Robertson.

Office for National Statistics (ONS). (2015). *Families and Households, 2014*. London: ONS.

Oliver, P. (2003). *Dwellings: The Vernacular House Worldwide*. London: Phaidon.

O'Sullivan, A., and Gibb, K. (2012). Housing taxation and the economic benefits of home-ownership. *Housing Studies*, 27(2): 267–79.

Pager, D., and Shepherd, H. (2008). The sociology of discrimination: Racial discrimination in employment, housing, credit, and consumer markets. *Annual Review of Sociology*, 34: 181.

Paris, C. (2008). Re-positioning second homes within housing studies: Household investment, gentrification, multiple residence, mobility and hyper construction. *Housing Theory and Society*, 4(2): 1–19.

Paris, C. (2010). *Affluence, Mobility and Second Home Ownership*. London: Routledge.

Park, R. (1928). Human migration and the marginal man. *American Journal of Sociology*, 22: 881–93.

Park, R., and Burgess, E. (1925/1967). *The City*. Chicago: University of Chicago Press.

Parker, S., Uprichard, E., and Burrows, R. (2007). Class places and place classes geodemographics and the spatialization of class. *Information, Communication and Society*, 10(6): 902–21.

Pawson, H. (2006). Restructuring England's social housing sector since 1989: Undermining or underpinning the fundamentals of public housing? *Housing Studies*, 21(5): 767–83.

Pawson, H., and Mullins, D. (2010). *After Council Housing: Britain's New Social Landlords*. Basingstroke: Palgrave Macmillan.

Peck, J. (2010). *Constructions of Neoliberal Reason*. New York: Oxford University Press.

Phillimore, J. (2013). Housing, home and neighbourhood renewal in the era of superdiversity: Some lessons from the West Midlands. *Housing Studies*, 28(5): 682–700.

Philo, G., Briant, E., and Donald, P. (2013). *Bad News for Refugees*. London: Pluto.

Piketty, T. (2014). *Capital in the 21st Century*. Cambridge, MA: Harvard University Press.

Pink, S. (2004). *Home Truths: Gender, Domestic Objects and Everyday Life*. Oxford: Berg.

Popkin, S., Katz, B., Cunningham, M., Brown, K., Gustafson, J. and Turner, M. (2004). *A Decade of Hope VI: Research Findings and Policy Challenges*. Washington: The Urban Institute/ The Brookings Institution.

Porteous, J. D., and Smith, S. (2001). *Domicide: The Global Destruction of Home*. Montreal: McGill-Queens.

Postman, N. (1992). *Technopoly*. New York: Knopf.

Pun, N. (2005). *Made in China*. Durham, NC: Duke University Press.

Putnam, R. (2007). E pluribus unum: Diversity and community in the twenty-first century: The 2006 Johan Skytte prize lecture. *Scandinavian Political Studies*, 30(2): 137–74.

Raco, M. (2013). *State-led Privatisation and the Demise of the Welfare State* Aldershot: Ashgate.

Rapoport, A. (2001). Theory, culture and housing. *Housing, Theory and Society*, 17(4): 145–65.

Ravetz, A. (2003). *Council Housing and Culture: The History of a Social Experiment*. London: Routledge.

Reuveny, R. (2007). Climate change-induced migration and violent conflict. *Political Geography*, 26(6): 656–73.

Rex, J., and Moore, R. (1967). *Race, Community and Conflict*. London: Oxford University Press.

Ritzer, G. (1988). *Sociological Theory*. New York: Alfred A. Knopf.

Roberts, M. (1991). *Living in a Man-made World: Gender Assumptions in Modern Housing Design*. London: Routledge.

Robinson, V., Hockey, J., and Meah, A. (2004). What I used to do . . . on my mother's settee: Spatial and emotional aspects of heterosexuality in England. *Gender, Place and Culture*, 11(3): 417–35.

Ronald, R. (2007). Comparing homeowner societies: Can we construct an East-West model? *Housing Studies*, 22(4): 473–93.

Rose, N. (2000). Government and control. *British Journal of Criminology*, 40: 321–29.

Rossen, L. M., Pollack, K. M., Curriero, F. C., Shields, T. M., Smart, M. J., Furr-Holden, C. D. M., and Cooley-Strickland, M. (2011). Neighborhood incivilities, perceived neighborhood safety, and walking to school among urban-dwelling children. *Journal of Physical Activity and Health*, 8(2): 262.

Rotker, S. (Ed.), (2002). *Citizens of Fear: Urban Violence in Latin America*. New Brunswick, NJ: Rutgers University Press.

Rowlands, R., and Gurney, C. M. (2000). Young peoples? Perceptions of housing tenure: A case study in the socialization of tenure prejudice. *Housing, Theory and Society*, 17(3): 121–30.

Roy, A. (2011). Slumdog cities: Rethinking subaltern urbanism. *International Journal of Urban and Regional Research*, 35(2): 223–38.

Ruonavaara, H. (1993). Types and forms of housing tenure: Towards solving the comparison/translation problem. *Scandinavian Housing and Planning Research*, 10(1): 3–20.

Ryan, L., and Mulholland, J. (2014). Trading places: French highly skilled migrants negotiating mobility and emplacement in London. *Journal of Ethnic and Migration Studies*, 40(4): 584–600.

Rykwert, J. (1991). House and home. *Social Research*, 58(1): 51–62.

Sassen, S. (2012). Expanding the terrain for global capital: When local housing becomes an electronic instrument. In M. B. Aalbers (Ed.), *Subprime Cities: The Political Economy of Mortgage Markets* (pp. 74–96). Oxford: Blackwell Publishing.

Satterthwaite, D., and Mitlin, D. (2013). *Reducing Urban Poverty in the Global South*. London: Routledge.

Saunders, P. (1990). *A Nation of Homeowners*. London: Allen and Unwin.

Saunders, P. (2007). *Social Theory and the Urban Question*. London: Routledge.

Saunders, P., and Williams, P. (1988). The constitution of the home: Towards a research agenda. *Housing Studies*, 3(2): 81–93.

Savage, M. (2000). *Class Analysis and Social Transformation*. Buckingham: Open University Press.

Savage, M. (2012). Broken communities? In W. Atkinson, S. Roberts, and M. Savage (Eds.), *Class Inequality in Austerity Britain* (pp. 145–62). Basingstoke: Palgrave Macmillan.

Savage, M., Bagnall, G., and Longhurst, B. (2005). *Globalisation and Belonging*. London: Sage.

Savage, M., and Warde, A. (1993). *Urban Sociology, Capitalism and Modernity*. Basingstoke: Macmillan.

Schwartz, A. (2010). *Housing Policy in the United States*. London and New York: Routledge.

Schwartz, A. (2012). US housing policy in the age of Obama: From crisis to stasis. *International Journal of Housing Policy*, 12(2): 227–40.

Shaw, K., and Hagemans, I. (2015). "Gentrification without displacement" and the consequent loss of place: The effects of class transition on low-income residents of secure housing in gentrifying areas. *International Journal of Urban and Regional Research*, 39(2): 323–41.

Shove, E. (2003). *Comfort, Cleanliness and Convenience: The Social Organization of Normality*. Oxford: Berg.

Shove, E., Watson, M., Hand, M., and Ingram, J. (2007). *The Design of Everyday Life*. Oxford: Berg.

Simpson, R. (2012). Households and families. In S. Smith, M. Elsinga, L. Fox O'Mahony, S. Ong, S. Wachter, and M. Eastaway (Eds.), *The International Encyclopedia of Housing and Home* (pp. 227–33). Amsterdam: Elsevier.

Skeggs, B. (2004). *Class, Self and Culture*. London: Routledge.

Slater, T. (2006). The eviction of critical perspectives from gentrification research. *International Journal of Urban and Regional Research*, 30(4): 737–57.

Smith, N., and LeFaivre, M. (1984). A class analysis of gentrification. In J. Palen and B. London, Gentrification, Displacement and Neighbourhood Revitalization (pp. 43–63). Albany, NY: State University of New York Press.

Smith, N. (1979). Toward a theory of gentrification; A back to the city movement of capital, not people. *Journal of the American Planning Association*, 45(4): 538–48.

Smith, N. (1995). *The New Urban Frontier: Gentrification and the Revanchist City*. London: Routledge.

Smith, N. (2005). *The Endgame of Globalization*. London: Routledge.

Smith, S. (2007). Owner occupation: At home with a hybrid of money and materials, *Environment and Planning A*, 40(3): 520–35.

Smith, S., and Munro, M. (2009). *The Microstructures of Housing Markets*. London: Routledge.

Smith, S., and Searle, B. (2008). Dematerialising money? Observations on the flow of wealth from housing to other things. *Housing Studies*, 23(1): 21–43.

Smith, S., Searle, B., and Cook, N. (2008). Rethinking the risks of homeownership. *Journal of Social Policy*, 38(1): 83–102.

Somerville, P. (1989). Home sweet home: A critical comment on Saunders and Williams. *Housing Studies*, 4(2): 113–18.

Somerville, P. (1997). The social construction of home. *Journal of Architectural and Planning Research*, 14(3): 226–45.

Standing, G. (2011). *The Precariat: The New Dangerous Class*. London: Bloomsbury Academic.

Stanko, E. (1990). *Everyday Violence*. London: HarperCollins.

Sullivan, O. (2004). Changing gender practices within the household: A theoretical perspective. *Gender and Society*, 18(2): 207–22.

Sumka, H. J. (1979). Neighbourhood revitalization and displacement. A review of the evidence. *Journal of the American Planning Association*, 45(4): 480–87.

Tanizaki, J. (2001). *In Praise of Shadows*. New York: Random House.

Tewdwr-Jones, M. (2011). *Urban Reflections: Narratives of Place, Planning and Change*. Bristol: Policy Press.

Therborn, G. (2013). *The Killing Fields of Inequality*. Cambridge: Polity.

Thomas, N. (1991). *Entangled Objects: Exchange, Material Culture, and Colonialism in the Pacific*. Cambridge, MA: Harvard University Press.

Thrift, N. (2007). *Non-Representational Theory, Space, Politics, Affect*. London: Routledge.

Tickamyer, A. (2000). Space matters! Spatial inequality in future sociology. *Contemporary Sociology*, 29(6): 805–13.

Torgersen, U. (1987). Housing: The wobbly pillar under the welfare state. *Scandinavian Housing and Planning Research*, 4(1): 116–26.

Tufte, V., and Myerhoff, B. G. (Eds.), (1979). *Changing Images of the Family*. New Haven, CT: Yale University Press.

UN Department of Economic and Social Affairs (UNDESA). (2002). *World Urbanization Prospects, The 2001 Revision*. New York: UNDESA.

United Nation's High Commissioner for Refugees (UNHCR). (2014). *2008 Global Trends: Forced Displacement*. Geneva: UNHCR.

Urry, J. (2000). *Sociology Beyond Societies: Mobilities for the Twenty-First Century*. New York and London: Routledge.

Van Dijk, J., Van Kesteren, J., and Smit, P. (2007). *Criminal Victimisation in International Perspective: Key Findings from the 2004–2005 ICVS and EU ICS*. The Hague: Ministry of Justice/ UNODC.

Venkatesh, S. A. (2000). *American Project: The Rise and Fall of a Modern Ghetto*. Cambridge, MA: Harvard University Press.

Wacquant, L. (2008). *Urban Outcasts*. Cambridge: Polity.

Walby, S., and Allan, J. (2004). *Domestic Violence, Sexual Assault and Stalking: Findings from the British Crime Survey*. London: Home Office.

Walker, A., Flatley, J., Kershaw, C., and Moon, D. (2009). *Crime in England and Wales 2008/09, Volume 1: Findings from the British Crime Survey and Police Recorded Crime*. London: Home Office.

Wallerstein, I. (1999). *The End of the World as We Know it: Social Science for the Twenty-First Century*. Minneapolis: University of Minnesota Press.

Warner, S. B. (1978). *Streetcar Suburbs: The Process of Growth in Boston, 1870–1900*. Cambridge, MA: Harvard University Press.

Watt, P. (2009). Housing stock transfers, regeneration and state-led gentrification in London. *Urban Policy and Research*, 27(3): 229–42.

Watt, P. (2013). It's not for us. *City: Analysis of Urban Trends, Culture, Theory, Policy, Action*, 17(1): 99–118.

Wilkinson, R., and Pickett, K. (2009). *The Spirit Level: Why Equality Is Better for Everyone*. London: Penguin.

Wills, J. (2008). Mapping class and its political possibilities. *Antipode*, 40(1): 25–30.

Wilson, W. (1987). *The Truly Disadvantaged: The Inner City, the Underclass and Public Policy*. Chicago: University of Chicago Press.

Wilson, W. (1996). *When Work Disappears: The World of the New Urban Poor*. New York: Knopf.

Winlow, S., and Hall, S. (2013). *Rethinking Social Exclusion: The End of the Social?* London: Sage.

Winnicott, D. W. (1965). *The Family and Individual Development*. Alameda, CA: Tavistock.

Wirth, L. (1947). Housing as a field of sociological research. *American Sociological Review*, 12(2), The American Family and Its Housing (April): 137–43.

Wolsink, M. (2006). Invalid theory impedes our understanding: A critique on the persistence of the language of NIMBY. *Transactions of the Institute of British Geographers*, 31(1): 85–91.

World Health Organization (WHO). (2014). *Child Maltreatment Fact Sheet no. 150*, Geneva: WHO.

World Health Organization (WHO) and United Nations International Children's Emergency Fund (UNICEF). (2006). Meeting the MDG Drinking Water and Sanitation Target: The Urban and Rural Challenge of the Decade. Geneva, Switzerland: WHO and UNICEF.

Wright, P. (1991). *Journey Through Ruins: The Last Days of London*. London: Radius Books.

Wu, F. (2012). Housing and the state in China. In S. Smith, M. Elsinga, L. Fox O'Mahony, S. Ong, S. Wachter, and M. Eastaway (Eds.), *The International Encyclopedia of Housing and Home* (pp. 323–29). Amsterdam: Elsevier.

Young, J. (2007). *The Vertigo of Late Modernity*. London: Sage.

Young, M., and Wilmott, P. (1957). *Family and Kinship in East London*. London: Routledge.

Zizek, S. (1989). *The Sublime Object of Ideology*. London: Verso.

Zizek, S. (2011). *Living in the End Times*. London: Verso.

Zukin, S. (1982). *Loft Living: Culture and Capital in Urban Change*. Baltimore, MD: Johns Hopkins University Press.

Index